WHAT EVERY GRIEVING MOTHER WISHES YOU KNEW

HOW TO SUPPORT, HEAL, AND REMEMBER TOGETHER

Janet Little Cooper

Published by: With My Father's Hands Publishing

Pensacola, Florida, USA

ISBN: 979-8-218-60613-8

Cover Design: PixelStudios

Interior Design: HMDPublishing

Edited by: Hailey Conor

Printed in the United States of America

Disclaimer:

This book is nonfiction, reflecting the author's personal experiences and interpretations.

Scripture References: Unless noted otherwise, Scripture quotations are from the *New International Version (NIV)*, ©1973, 1978, 1984, 2011 by Biblica, Inc. Used with permission.

PUBLISHING

With My Father's Hands was founded to honor both the legacy of my earthly father and the eternal presence of my Heavenly Father. Through the handwritten sermons written by my father, Rev. Thomas Little, Jr., which he left to me when he passed in 2016, his words continue to teach, encourage, and inspire.

Just as my father's hands once penned messages of truth and wisdom, and just as God's hands have guided me and sustained me in life and this book, this name represents a mission to carry forward that same calling of sharing words that uplift, strengthen, and bring light to those who read them.

Connect With Me

a www.amazon.com/author/Janet Little Cooper

✉ withmyfathershands@gmail.com

f Janet Little Cooper or Life According to Janet

○ www.instagram.com/by_janetlittlecooper

♪ www.tiktok.com/@janet.cooper7

In memory of my precious son, Bryant.

Your strength, faith, and unwavering love inspire me daily. I will carry you in my heart until the day we are reunited.

Dedicated to my son Austin. Your strength, love, and unwavering support have carried me when I couldn't stand alone. You are a testament to resilience and a reminder that love endures all things.

CONTENTS

Preface _____ 6

THE WEIGHT OF GRIEF

01. A Mother's Last Goodbye _____ 9
02. The Sacred Drive _____ 12
03. When Your Child Plans Their Goodbye _____ 14
04. Diagnosis Day _____ 18
05. A Lifetime of Loss _____ 23
06. Grief Has Many Faces_____ 29
07. The Definition of Grief_____ 32
08. The Weight of Guilt & Regret In Grief _____ 35
09. The Isolation of Grief_____ 39

WRESTLING WITH GRIEF AND FAITH

10. What Not To Say_____ 44
11. Please Say Their Name _____ 50
12. When Faith Feels Fragile _____ 53
13. From Faith to Fury _____ 58
14. The Right to Grieve Publicly _____ 62
15. Practical Ways to Help_____ 66

PAIN, PURPOSE, AND PEACE

16. When the Holidays Hurt _____ 72
17. When Living Feels Impossible _____ 77
18. Impact of Grief On Marriage _____ 82
19. Siblings: The Silent Survivors _____ 89
20. A Bond Forged In Grief _____ 94
21. Music in the Night_____ 98

LIVING WITH LOSS

22. My Dad's Sermons_____ 103
23. Peace in Complete Healing _____ 111
24. Finding Joy _____ 114
25. Finding Freedom in Forgiveness _____ 118
26. You Truly Aren't Alone _____ 122
27. Scripture for the Journey _____ 128
28. Encouragement for the Brokenhearted _____ 133
29. Bryant's Greatest Hope _____ 137

MEMORIES IN PICTURES

Acknowledgments _____ 158

Preface

A Book for Everyone Who Has Faced Loss

Grief has a way of making you feel like you're walking through life with a shattered heart, unsure if it will ever feel whole again. When my son **Bryant Thomas Cooper,** 19, took his last breath, it felt like time stopped. Not long before that, I had already lost my parents. Each loss layered my grief until I felt as though I was drowning in it. If you are reading this, you have likely experienced loss, too. Let me say this first: I am so sorry for your loss.

You will see the words "You are not alone" often in this book, and specific scriptures are printed more than once. When I was in the darkest valleys of my grief, I used to hate hearing those words. People often said it to comfort me, reminding me that God was with me. But in the moment, I felt only the crushing reality of my loneliness. I was divorced. My parents were gone. My son was gone. In my eyes, I couldn't have been more alone than I was.

And yet, in hindsight, those four words carried a truth I couldn't see then. They planted a seed of assurance in my heart that, on some of my darkest days, gave me the strength to keep going. I wasn't truly alone. God was there, and over time, I realized He was working through the people around me—friends, family, even strangers—who showed up in ways I didn't always notice until later. Those four words hold a lot of weight in grief.

WHAT EVERY GRIEVING MOTHER WISHES YOU KNEW

While this book is deeply rooted in my experience as a mother who lost her son, it is not just for parents who have lost children. It's for anyone who has lost a loved one or even a dream. Grief doesn't always come from death—it can come from the loss of a relationship, a career, a home, or a future you once envisioned. Loss comes in many forms, and so does the healing journey. No matter what kind of loss you have faced, this book reminds you that grief is universal, and so is the hope that can follow.

This book is for you, dear reader, because I know the weight of grief, the questions, the anger, and the loneliness that come with it. It's a journey I never wanted to take, and I imagine you feel the same. But together, we can walk this road with honesty, faith, and the hope that healing—though slow—will come.

PART ONE

THE WEIGHT OF GRIEF

Chapter One
A MOTHER'S LAST GOODBYE

"I told him it was okay to go, though my heart screamed for him to stay."

The hospital room was silent, except for the stark shift in my son's breathing. The loud, labored sound pulled me from sleep. It was the morning after Thanksgiving—Black Friday—a day that had always thrilled my son, Bryant. As a child, he eagerly joined my brother, **Jeffrey Little**, for Black Friday shopping, chasing deals and sharing laughter. In a bittersweet way, it felt almost fitting that Bryant's 25-month battle with cancer would end on a day that had once brought him so much joy.

Bryant was now unresponsive. The night before Thanksgiving, I had heard his frail, hoarse voice whisper, "I love you" for the last time. I held his hand tightly, singing the little songs he loved when he was scared or felt terrible, whispering how much I loved him. I told him it was okay to go, though my heart screamed for him to stay. He never opened his eyes, but the firm squeeze of his hand told me he knew I was there—that he understood every word.

Beckie Nelson, my dear friend, and a fellow grieving mother, had stayed with us through Thanksgiving night, unwilling to let us face this alone. As two of Bryant's nurses moved quietly around us, Beckie did something only someone who had walked this path before could genuinely understand. She laid her body over mine, completely enveloping me in warmth and pressure as if shielding me from the unbearable pain that was about to come. She not only anticipated what was coming but understood it in a way only another grieving mother could.

Bryant took his last breath that morning. In that instant, a grief so immense and consuming crashed over me that no words could ever capture its depth. Beckie's body pressed firmly against mine, anchoring me to the bed as the raw, guttural cries of my shattered heart poured from my mouth.

For a long time, I had suppressed my tears in front of Bryant because they frightened him and made him sad. He had already endured too much loss. My mother, **Joyce Little**, had died of cancer just seven months after his diagnosis, and my father, **Rev. Thomas Little**, followed her seven months later. Their deaths had nearly swallowed me whole, dragging me into the suffocating depths of grief.

I hadn't truly understood Bryant's plea for me not to cry in front of him—until I heard my father weep after my mother passed. The sound of his sorrow was unbearable, a pain so sharp it carved into my soul. Only then did I grasp why Bryant had asked me to shield him from my tears. I honored his request, muffling my sobs beneath layers of blankets and pillows or slipping into another room to grieve in silence.

My sweet baby boy was gone. His hard-fought battle with cancer had come to an end.

The Shadows of Loss

When Bryant was four, his cousin, **Reagan Reid Little**, died suddenly from viral meningitis. It happened in a whirlwind—three devastating days from the first symptoms to the unimaginable loss. Bryant was too young to comprehend what had happened. To him, Reagan was more than just a cousin—she was his person. They were inseparable, bound by a love so deep and instinctive that no one else could fully understand it.

Years later, Bryant would make countless trips to the ER for asthma attacks and allergic reactions. Each time I loaded him into the car, he would cry, pleading with me not to leave him in the hospital the way Aunt Deb had left Reagan. That fear never left him. Because of that, I promised him I would never leave him behind.

When Bryant passed away, **Erin Shipp Contreras**, the hospital's Child Life Specialist, honored our requests. As a cancer survivor herself, she understood—perhaps better than anyone—why those details mattered. Because of her efforts, Bryant was never taken to the hospital morgue. Instead, the funeral home owners, longtime family friends, were called to retrieve his body. For two years, Bryant and I had always left the hospital together, and this final time would be no different.

The Final Journey

With his body carefully covered, we left the hospital—Bryant on a gurney, a stark contrast to 25 years earlier when I was wheeled out of that same building cradling my firstborn son, **Austin Cooper**, in my arms. That painful symmetry wasn't lost on me as I walked beside one son who was alive and another who no longer drew breath.

Beckie drove me as we followed the vehicle carrying Bryant's body on his final trip from Pensacola to the funeral home. I didn't want to leave him there. I wanted to stay with him. But I wasn't allowed.

For nearly two years, Bryant and I had spent almost every waking second together, battling cancer side by side. Now, suddenly, I was without him. Even though I knew he was no longer in his body, the separation was unbearable.

The Weight of Grief

I was divorced from Bryant's dad and lived next door to my parents, who were now gone. My oldest son, Austin, was in Pensacola, so I felt utterly alone in those early days after Bryant's passing. Beckie stayed with me. Again, only she truly understood the significance of presence in the depths of grief. She drove me to the funeral home the next day to make Bryant's arrangements and remained by my side until my brothers and their families arrived.

I had been with Beckie during the tragic loss of her only son, **Travis Nelson**—a 19-year-old Marine in 2011. It was devastating beyond words. But at that time, I never imagined I would one day be walking in those same shoes.

The same was true for my niece, Reagan. Never, in my worst nightmares, did I think our family would endure such a horrific loss. Our father had suffered a massive heart attack at 47, and for so long, we braced ourselves against the possibility of losing him early due to his heart condition.

We never imagined that sweet, innocent Reagan would be the first to leave us. And after losing her, we certainly never believed it possible to lose another child in our family. But we did. And our family would never be the same.

Chapter 2
THE SACRED DRIVE

"Bryant was telling me he was ready, and I knew it was time to let go."

Bryant was in bad shape—his body swollen from steroids, confined to a wheelchair, his voice barely a whisper as the tumor pressed against his throat. Yet, even in his suffering, his spirit remained unbroken.

We had just crossed the toll bridge onto Pensacola Beach after another exhausting day of scans and a doctor's appointment. The weight of it all pressed down on me as I drove, but then Bryant broke the silence with words that stopped my heart.

"Mom, you know my body is never going to be normal again until I go to Heaven," he said quietly.

My heart plummeted.

Bryant had told me many times that he was dying, but each time, I had managed to dodge the conversation—clinging to the fragile hope that we still had time. But at that moment, I couldn't hide from the truth any longer. And for the first time, I found the strength to say the words I had been too afraid to speak.

"I know, son," I whispered, my voice trembling, my eyes brimming with tears.

As sick as he was, Bryant turned to me and gave me one of his radiant, beautiful smiles that somehow conveyed peace despite everything he was enduring. Something shifted inside me.

For two years, we had fought together—clinging to every treatment, every hope, every chance. But now, Bryant was telling me he was ready. And I knew it was time to let go.

I took a deep breath and continued, *"I love you so much, Bryant, and I'm so sorry you've had to suffer like this. But I want you to know how proud I am of you."* My voice wavered, but I pressed on. *"I don't know what Heaven will be like, but from everything I've been taught and everything I've read, I know this—you won't be in pain anymore. Your legs will work again, and your voice will be strong. There is no time in Heaven,"* I added gently. *"You won't miss me or Austin or Dad. Before you know it, we'll be there with you, just like we were never apart. And you'll be with Granny, Papa, Reagan, Grandma, Papa Lawrence, Travis, Mr. Scott, Kena, Johann, Rachel, and Jace. There are so many people in heaven who love you and they will be there waiting for you. You won't be scared or alone."*

His smile stretched from ear to ear. He didn't say a word. He didn't have to. That peaceful, joyful smile took my breath away.

I knew what I had to say next would break our hearts, but I needed him to hear it. *"I know you don't like to see or hear me cry,"* I said, trembling. *"But when you leave for Heaven, I am going to cry—probably a lot—because I love you so much, and I'll miss you terribly. But I promise you, I will be okay eventually."*

I don't remember the rest of the drive. I don't even remember pulling into the condo parking lot. All I remember is the presence of God in that car with us. He was there—guiding my words, holding us both.

When we arrived at the condo, I went to the trunk to get Bryant's wheelchair. As I was lifting it out, my phone rang. It was Bryant's oncologist.

"The tumors in Bryant's liver have grown so large that they are blocking the small bile ducts," he said. His voice was calm but direct, delivering the news I had dreaded for months. *"It won't be long now. He may have a week left. There is nothing more we can do other than keep him comfortable."*

I wanted to scream. To cry. To collapse under the weight of it all. But I couldn't. Bryant was waiting in the car, and I had to be strong. I never told him about the doctor's call.

The following morning, everything had changed. Bryant was unresponsive. I shook him gently, calling his name, but he didn't stir. I had known this moment was coming, but knowing and living it are two entirely different things.

Panic surged through me as I called for help. My heart was racing as it dropped to my toes.

When the firefighters arrived, they carefully lifted him from the bed onto a gurney. I followed behind them as they carried him to the ambulance, my heart pounding, knowing we were nearing the end of his journey.

I called the oncology nurse's station to let them know we were on our way. And just like that, Bryant's wishes for his final moments were put into motion.

Chapter 3
WHEN YOUR CHILD PLANS THEIR GOODBYE

"When the time comes, do you want to be at home with Hospice, or do you want to be here in the hospital?"

Austin's voice was thick with concern while talking to me on the phone, his voice edged with exhaustion. His four-month-old baby girl, Ava Jane, was sick for the first time—RSV (Respiratory Syncytial Virus) and an ear infection. Nothing seemed to comfort her.

"I love her being a baby," he said, *"but I can't wait for her to get older so I don't worry about her as much."*

I smiled, shaking my head at his innocence as a first-time father.

"Son, I hate to tell you—the worry doesn't go away. Ever." He listened quietly as I continued. *"No matter Ava's age, you'll always worry about her being sick or going through something hard. You're 32, and I still worry about you. I pray for you every single day, asking God to protect you. Your concern for your child doesn't lessen as they grow—it only gets stronger."*

He made a slight sound—as if he was accepting my words—but I knew he didn't fully understand. Not yet. He wouldn't, not until the day he faced something he had no control over.

Once, I believed I could protect my two boys from anything. But nothing prepares you for the moment your child looks you in the eye and tells you how they want to die.

The Moment Everything Changed

Bryant had fought hard. But there came a day when he decided he was done. The chemotherapy wasn't buying him any more time—it was only stripping away what little quality of life he had left. His body was exhausted, and at just 18 years old, he decided on his own to stop treatment.

It wasn't a choice made lightly, but it was his to make. Once he decided, his doctors, nurses, and caregivers began to prepare.

I will never forget that day in the hospital when they gathered in his room— the lead doctor, his primary nurse, the child life specialist, and the chaplain. They sat with him and, with unimaginable gentleness, asked the most challenging question a person can ever hear.

"When the time comes, do you want to be at home with Hospice, or do you want to be here in the hospital?"

Bryant didn't hesitate. *"The hospital."*

He wanted to be in a place where he felt safe, knew he'd be cared for, and— most of all—where he wouldn't be a burden to me. And because he was legally an adult, these choices were entirely his.

From that moment forward, he began making the plans no child should ever have to make.

The Plans of an 18-Year-Old Who Trusted God Completely

He chose his hospital room. He had a specific room in mind, but when the time came, it was occupied. Instead, he was placed in the same room where he had received his very first chemotherapy treatment—precisely 25 months to the day. It wasn't a coincidence. It felt as if God and Bryant had orchestrated it together from the very beginning.

He also had a special request. He asked for a bariatric bed wider than a standard hospital bed so I could be beside him when he needed comfort the most. In the end, I only got to do that for one night. His tumors had grown so large that even the lightest touch became unbearable. When I could no longer hold him, the nurses pushed his bed right up against the bench where I slept, lowering the rail so I could still be as close as possible without causing him pain. Even in his suffering, he sought comfort. And God provided it.

He hand-picked his nurses. He didn't want just anyone caring for him in his final days. He carefully selected two nurses for the day and two for the night shifts. They would be the only ones tending to him, ensuring he was surrounded by people he trusted. These nurses weren't just random caregivers. Each of them had walked this journey with him from the very beginning. They had witnessed his struggle and unwavering faith and had cared for him as if he were family. Before we realized we would need them, God had already placed them in our lives.

He made a list of the foods and drinks he wanted, though he was too sick to eat or drink when the time came. Still, his team graciously anticipated his every need.

Then, he made the most challenging choice of all—he did not want to be placed on life support. No ventilators, no desperate attempts to prolong his time beyond what his body could endure. He signed a Do Not Resuscitate (DNR) order with determination.

That was the moment that shattered me. No parent should ever have to watch their child sign their death order. Nor should a parent have to make that heartbreaking decision on their behalf.

Years earlier, my brother and his wife had faced the unbearable decision to take their daughter, Reagan, off life support. At the time, I couldn't have imagined what that moment felt like. But now, I had seen it firsthand—the dreadful, horrific moments before they returned to her room, carrying the weight of that final choice.

And no mother should ever have to sit in silence, choking back sobs, as her child makes the most gut-wrenching decision of their life. But I did.

And Bryant? He never wavered. His peace was steadfast. His faith was unshaken because he knew—without a doubt—that his healing was coming.

Not here. Not in the way we had hoped. But in the way God had always intended—through Heaven.

The Question That Shattered Us

Bryant and I had already come to terms with the reality of his prognosis, knowing the nature of his cancer. Early in his battle, we sat in a conference room with Bryant's oncologist in Pensacola to discuss the treatment plan set by his specialist in Houston. Several other members of his medical team were also gathered around the table.

The oncologist explained the extent of the cancer spreading inside him and outlined the next steps. I can't recall exactly what she said that prompted Bryant's question. All I remember is her response.

Bryant looked at her and asked, "What happens next?"

Without hesitation, she answered—boldly and with certainty—"The process of dying begins."

I remember feeling his body shift next to mine. Bryant didn't panic. He didn't cry. He processed her words. I won't say he wasn't afraid—how could he not be?

But I will say this: He never lost faith.

In that moment, he had two choices:

1. To be consumed by fear.
2. To trust the God who had walked with him every step of the way.

Bryant chose faith. And in the following months, I watched my son walk toward eternity with his head held high. He had his tear-filled moments, sharing his fears and regrets with me and others. He was, after all, still a teenage boy. But he carried the courage of a giant and a heart like Jesus.

God Was in Every Detail

Looking back, I see it all so clearly. From the moment of his diagnosis to his very last breath, God was in every detail. He had been there from the beginning—since Bryant's birth.

The timing. Precisely 25 months—to the day.

The hospital room. The same one where he fought his first battle.

The nurses. The ones who loved him as if he were their own.

The faith. Unshaken.

Nothing was accidental. None of it was random. Bryant's life, his fight, his final days—it was as if he and God had sat down together and mapped out every moment. And though it shattered me, though it broke every part of me to let him go, I knew one thing with absolute certainty: God was carrying him home.

It all began with a single moment.

One doctor's words.

One reality that shattered everything I thought I knew about life.

Diagnosis Day. That was where the fight began, where the road to this moment had started. Where God first took Bryant's hand—and never let go. And that's where the next chapter begins.

Chapter 4
DIAGNOSIS DAY

"Those doctors can't number my days. Only God can."

I often look back on that first day—**October 27, 2014**—the day Bryant's diagnosis changed our lives forever. And I wish I could rewrite it. I wish I could go back and stop what was coming. But that's the thing about life—you don't always see the storms until you're standing in the middle.

Thankfully, I've learned that **God always goes ahead of us.** Every detail of our journey was filtered through His hands long before we knew what we were facing.

Bryant was **seventeen** when he first noticed something wasn't right. He began complaining of lower back pain—pain that seemed far too intense for a healthy, active teenage boy. At first, we thought he had injured himself while working at **Smith Tractor, a local John Deere dealership.** But the pain didn't go away. It only got worse.

After five days of unrelenting pain, I made an appointment for Bryant with his pediatrician, **Dr. Marian B. Stewart-Griffin.** Several hours before his appointment, he showed up unexpectedly at *The Tri-City Ledger,* where I worked as the managing editor of the weekly newspaper. Bryant's face was pale as a ghost, drenched in sweat, and he was doubled over in pain.

"I can't wait," he told me.

I called Dr. Stewart on her cell. She told me to get him to the emergency room immediately. We both thought it was kidney stones. We were so sure of it.

But after the ER doctor read the scans and tests, the look on her face told me everything.

Something was wrong.

Bad wrong.

Finally, the words came—words no mother ever wants to hear.

"We found four tumors in your son's liver. It looks like cancer."

My heart dropped. I wanted to scream, to run, to bargain with God. **This couldn't be happening—especially not to Bryant.**

Maybe it was instinct for me, working as a journalist, to start hurling a barrage of questions with absolute clarity to the unfamiliar ER doctor as we waited for Bryant's pediatrician to arrive.

What kind of cancer?

How bad is it?

What's the treatment plan?

However, my tone and attitude showed that I was a protective mother above all else. I told her she was wrong and had no idea what she was saying. I was in complete denial. In hindsight, there is no way she could answer the questions I demanded she give me immediate answers for.

Thankfully, Dr. Stewart's swift response to my frantic call to get to the ER calmed me as she looked at the scans. She saw the same thing the ER doctor saw, but I wasn't as aggressive with her because I trusted her. Within no time, we were scheduled to visit an oncologist in less than 24 hours—a process that could have taken weeks without her. That day had started like any other Monday. But by the time we left the ER, our world had shattered.

The Diagnosis That Changed Everything

We met with an oncologist at Pensacola's only children's hospital the following day. After a more in-depth scan, the doctor returned to the room carrying a box of Kleenex, tears welling in her eyes.

My heart sank. **I'm sure Bryant's did, too.** We had hoped that this was all a mistake, that it was nothing more than kidney stones.

But there was no mistake.

And there were no kidney stones.

Instead, the scan confirmed there were four tumors in Bryant's liver that appeared to be cancerous.

We were admitted to the hospital immediately. Nine excruciating days filled with relentless testing followed—Bryant being poked and prodded more than ever. Each day brought more images, more scans, and more tests.

Except for one.

Bryant tearfully asked his doctor if he could skip all tests for one day. She obliged.

That day, his hospital room overflowed with friends. They watched movies and hung out like normal teenagers.

But we all knew—**Bryant's life was far from normal anymore.**

After two liver biopsies, doctors finally told us on day 9 that it was Neuroendocrine carcinoma, a rare and aggressive cancer that primarily affects older men. Bryant's cancer had already spread and was given the classification of Stage 4.

Of four oncologists in Pensacola, only one had ever heard of it but never treated it. They began to confer with other hospitals. St. Jude was the first, but they wouldn't see Bryant because that type of cancer is known as being incurable. M.D. Anderson in Houston was the second call, and they agreed to see Bryant in two days. Bryant was released, and a local organization, **Pilots for Christ**, in Monroeville, AL, gifted us a free flight to Texas for his appointment. The Christian non-profit organization flew us to and from Houston on at least three different appointments.

The news we got in Houston was shocking—how it was presented even more so. The doctor explained the rarity of this cancer in adolescents and said he had only ever treated three cases. Bryant would make four. He told us the three previous patients had died.

"It is rare and has no cure, but we can get you started on a chemotherapy regimen that will prolong your life. Hopefully, it will help you keep kicking the can down the road for maybe two more years."

But Bryant was strong. He didn't cry, then, at least. He didn't panic—instead, that night, as we lay in bed in a Houston hotel, Bryant confidently said these words:

"Mom, I know you are scared, but those doctors can't number my days. Only God can."

I wish I could say I felt the same strength, but inside, I was terrified. I couldn't lose Bryant—I wouldn't.

A New Reality

The next few weeks blurred into a whirlwind of doctor's appointments, chemotherapy schedules, and hospital stays. Bryant's life—**our lives—were**

turned upside down. I left my job at the newspaper the same Monday I rushed Bryant to the ER. Nothing else mattered but being by my son's side.

I slept in hospital chairs, learned how to monitor his meds, and tried to stay one step ahead of the endless side effects and complications that came with treatment. I studied everything I could about his cancer, determined to find the best doctor for him. Eventually, I did. I found a specialist in New Orleans at Ochsner, whose entire practice focused on Bryant's type of cancer. That's when we learned it was the same cancer that took Apple mogul Steve Jobs life. Later, famous singer Aretha Franklin died from the same cancer, too.

Some people were able to live with it for 20-plus years, managing a low-grade form of the disease. But Bryant's case was different.

Stage 4. Highly aggressive.

70% out of 100%.

Bryant would continue receiving chemo in the Pensacola hospital. The Texas and New Orleans doctors agreed—it was best for him to stay close to home, surrounded by the people he loved. Every three months, we would travel to New Orleans for specialized care.

Yet, despite everything, **Bryant stayed positive.** He cracked jokes with the nurses, made friends with other patients, and somehow, through it all, held onto his faith—even when the pain was unbearable. His faith amazed me. Even as **mine wavered**—as I questioned why God would let my baby suffer—**Bryant stood tall.**

Leaning on Faith

But it wasn't easy. Watching Bryant suffer broke me in ways words could never fully capture. The treatments were brutal, and the side effects were relentless. And yet, through it all, Bryant kept smiling. I remember one day in particular—he was exhausted, his body weak from chemo, yet he still found the strength to encourage another struggling patient.

That was Bryant.

Even in his most challenging moments, he thought of others. As the oldest patient in the Oncology Unit, he was beloved by the nurses and a favorite among the younger children.

A Mother's Strength

Being a caregiver isn't just about physical care. It's emotional, spiritual, and fighting battles no one sees—the late nights, the quiet prayers, the desperate hope that somehow, some way, things will get better. I wish I could say I never questioned God. But I did. There were moments when I pleaded, "Why him? Why us?"

Yet, even in my doubts, Bryant's faith carried us both. And I knew—I had to keep believing even when the odds were stacked against us.

Encouragement to Other Mothers

If you've ever heard the words, **"Your child has cancer,"** you know the fear that follows—**a fear that grips your heart and refuses to let go.**

To the mothers walking this road right now—I see you.

I know your fear.

I know your exhaustion.

I know the questions that keep you up at night.

But I also know this: **God sees you. He hears your cries.**

And even when it feels like your world is falling apart—**He is holding you together.**

No matter how impossible it feels, **you can keep going.**

One step. One prayer. One breath at a time.

Chapter 5
A LIFETIME OF LOSS

"Mom, promise me I'm not going to die like Granny did."

L oss didn't begin with Bryant's cancer diagnosis. Grief had already become a familiar presence in my life long before that day in the hospital. By the time Bryant's battle began, I had endured more loss than I ever thought one person could bear.

Early Losses: My Grandparents

Some of my earliest experiences with grief came from losing my grandparents. One by one, beginning at age 12, I said goodbye to all four of them— each loss leaving an indelible mark on my heart.

They were the foundation of our family, **pillars of faith and love.** Losing them felt like losing pieces of myself. Their deaths taught me what it meant to grieve, but nothing could have prepared me for the heartbreak that would follow.

Losing My Niece—Reagan's Death

When Bryant was four years old, we experienced another devastating loss— one that would change the way he viewed illness and hospitals for the rest of his life.

My niece, Reagan, **passed away unexpectedly at just seven years old from viral meningitis.** It happened so fast—just three days from the first symptoms to her passing.

We were flown from Florida to Louisiana to say our goodbyes in Hal Sutton, my brother's former boss, a former champion golfer's private plane. Bryant couldn't pronounce the 'S' in Hal's last name and never said his name without saying his full name, which always came out as "Hal Wutton." Everyone loved hearing Bryant say it. I feel certain Hal still remembers that and the drive from the hospital to my brother's home.

I'll never forget walking into that hospital and seeing my oldest brother, **Gilbert Little,** his wife, **Deb**, and their daughter, **Meredith**, surrounded by friends and family. The hallways were lined with people who had come to pray and support them.

There wasn't a dry eye in the building.

Bryant didn't understand. He was too young to comprehend what was happening. All he knew was that Reagan was his best friend—his buddy—and now she was gone.

In the days, weeks, and months that followed, Bryant cried **countless** tears, unable to understand everything. He asked endless questions about why Reagan wasn't coming home with us and why Aunt Deb had to leave her behind in the hospital.

Facing the Fear of Hospitals

That experience shaped him in ways I couldn't have imagined.

After Reagan died, Bryant became terrified of hospitals. Every time he had to go to the ER, he would cry and beg me not to leave him behind the way Aunt Deb had "left" Reagan.

It broke my heart to see that fear in his eyes. I promised him over and over again that I would never leave him.

And I didn't.

Even during his cancer battle, I stayed by his side every second I could. When Bryant passed, I made sure the hospital honored our request that his body never go to the morgue—a promise I made to him. We left the hospital together for the final time—just as we always had.

Losing Travis—A Friend and Hero

In August of 2011, tragedy struck again with the death of Beckie's son Travis. Travis Nelson, a Marine, had just turned 19 while serving in the Helmand Province of Afghanistan. His unit came under attack during a routine patrol when an Afghan sniper shot Travis. He continued to fight, saving several members of his unit before he died. Travis was our neighbor and classmate with Austin. They, along with Bryant, became close friends. Travis felt like one of my own; the same could be said for Beckie and my boys. We were always together.

Travis wasn't just a hero in the military—he was a hero to everyone who knew him. He had a heart full of courage, kindness, and humor unlike any I'd ever witnessed. His death in Afghanistan shook our entire community.

Bryant looked up to Travis, and his death hit him hard. It was the second time Bryant had experienced the loss of someone close to his age and someone he loved dearly.

I stood beside Beckie, Travis's mother, as she faced the unthinkable—burying her only son. I watched her grieve with strength and grace, but I also saw the raw, soul-deep pain that only another grieving mother could understand.

I never imagined walking that same road just a few years later. But before that, Beckie's husband, Scott, died of cancer just one year and one month after their son's death. Around the same time, three years later, Scott's son and Beckie's stepson, Daniel, died as a result of an accident. Her father also died. Beckie and her young daughter, Anna, were left to grieve, mourn, and navigate a new life without the most important men who had once been in their lives.

Losing My Parents—The Final Blow Before Bryant's Death

As if losing Reagan hadn't been enough for our family, grief struck again—twice—in the months following Bryant's diagnosis.

My mom, Joyce Little, passed away from cancer just seven months after Bryant's diagnosis. I will never forget standing at her funeral, watching my son—bald from chemo—break down in tears just moments before the service began.

"Mom, promise me I'm not going to die like Granny did."

Seventeen months later, he did, exactly like my mom.

At the time, my heart had only the faintest clue of the depths of pain I would come to know.

And then, another devastating blow.

Just seven months after my mother's passing, my father—her husband of over fifty years—was gone, too. She had fought cancer for three years; my dad's body succumbed to heart disease. Losing both of them so close together nearly broke me.

My father was a Southern Baptist pastor. After he passed away in 2016, I inherited one of his most treasured possessions—his handwritten sermons. I remember holding the worn pages, running my fingers over his handwriting, and feeling an overwhelming connection to him.

I've spent hours trying to organize the hundreds of sermons by topic. Reading his words—his thoughts on faith, suffering, and hope—felt like he was still with me, speaking into the darkest valley of my life.

But at the time, I didn't know those losses were only the beginning of an even harder journey.

Bryant's Diagnosis—A New Wave of Grief

By the time we learned Bryant had cancer, grief already felt like my constant companion. I'd barely had time to catch my breath from losing my parents before I was thrust into another nightmare. I faced the possibility of losing my child.

I remember sitting in the hospital room with Bryant, watching him sleep, feeling completely helpless. I wanted to protect him, to take the cancer from him and carry it myself. But I couldn't.

Instead, I did the only thing I knew how to do: pray. I prayed for healing, strength, and time, and I prayed for God to carry us both because I knew I couldn't do it alone.

Through all my losses, I've come to understand that grief is not one-size-fits-all. Every loss is unique, shaped by the circumstances surrounding it, but the ache of losing someone you love is universal. For mothers, the pain of losing a child is something no one should have to bear alone.

As I reflect on my journey, I can't help but think about the many other mothers who have walked similar roads, each carrying their grief. Their stories remind me that while our paths may differ, the bond of shared loss can unite us in a way few others can understand.

Encouragement to Other Mothers and People Grieving

Grief has a way of piling up. It doesn't always come one loss at a time. Sometimes, it comes in waves, crashing into you before you've had time to recover from the last hit.

If you're facing layer upon layer of loss, I want you to know this: feeling overwhelmed, broken, and unsure of how to keep going is okay. But I also

WHAT EVERY GRIEVING MOTHER WISHES YOU KNEW

want you to know this—you don't have to carry it all alone. God sees your pain and is unafraid of your questions, anger, or tears. He doesn't expect you to have it all together.

He asks you to keep trusting Him—even when it feels impossible.

Isaiah 41:10 says: *"So do not fear, for I am with you; do not be dismayed, for I am your God. I will strengthen you and help you; I will uphold you with my righteous right hand."*

When the weight of grief feels too heavy, let God carry it for you. Know that even in your darkest moments, He is right there—holding, strengthening, and reminding you that you are never alone.

My brother Gilbert and his family before Reagan died.

WHAT EVERY GRIEVING MOTHER WISHES YOU KNEW

Chapter 6
GRIEF HAS MANY FACES

Grief is universal, but it wears many faces. Every parent who has lost a child knows the unbearable pain of absence—the hole in their heart where their child should be. However, the circumstances surrounding a child's death can shape the grieving process in ways as unique as the children themselves.

Some mothers lose a child they never get to hold due to a miscarriage or stillbirth. Their arms ache for a baby they felt in their hearts and bodies but never had the chance to cradle. The world often doesn't fully recognize their grief because there are no photos, no memories, no milestones. But that doesn't make their pain any less real.

Other mothers lose a child suddenly in an accident, a car crash, or a tragedy that takes their child away in an instant. The shock of such a loss leaves them reeling, unable to prepare or say goodbye. One moment, their world was whole; the next, it was shattered.

Some mothers endure the pain of having their child's life stolen through murder or violence. Their grief is compounded by anger, questions, and the unbearable knowledge that someone deliberately took their child away.

Not everyone thinks of the parents who grieve the loss of a child who isn't deceased but, due to heart-wrenching circumstances, are estranged from them. This separation comes for many reasons, but drug abuse is often the most common. This type of loss isn't always recognized as a loss but instead puts the parents in a negative, shameful light.

And then, there are mothers like me who lose a child after a long illness. We are the mothers who walk alongside our children through every stage of their suffering. We witness their bodies weaken, their smiles fade, and their hopes waver. We fight, advocate for them, and hold onto every moment, even as we see the inevitable approaching.

Losing Bryant to cancer after a 25-month battle was a grief that built over time. It is known as anticipatory grief. In some ways, it felt like a slow-motion car crash. I could see the wreck coming, but I couldn't stop it. I had time to say goodbye and prepare, yet no amount of time could ever truly prepare me to let him go.

What makes this kind of loss unique is the way grief mingles with exhaustion. I wasn't just grieving Bryant's death; I was grieving the years stolen from his life and the toll the illness had taken on both of us. I was physically, emotionally, and spiritually drained from the fight.

But as much as my experience is unique, I have learned something important: grief is not a competition.

The pain of losing a child cannot be measured or compared. Whether your child's death was sudden or drawn out, whether they were taken by illness, violence, or an accident, the ache of their absence is the same. It's a lifelong journey of learning to live with a hole in your heart.

I hope others will understand that each loss type has its challenges. If a mother loses her child suddenly, she doesn't have time to say goodbye. If a mother loses her child after a long illness, she has to live with the painful memories of watching her child suffer. If a mother loses her child through miscarriage or stillbirth, she has to fight to have her grief acknowledged in a world that often does not recognize it as a valid loss.

As grieving mothers, we carry these unique burdens. But what unites us is the shared bond of knowing our lives will never be the same. We don't need to compare our pain; we need to support one another through it.

If you are walking alongside a grieving mother, let her tell you her story. Please don't assume you understand her grief or try to compare it to someone else's. Every loss is unique. Every loss is devastating.

The progression of Bryant's beautiful smile is framed by the sweetest dimples! The milkshake picture was always a favorite. He had just been released from the ER at the same hospital he died in.

Chapter 7
THE DEFINITION OF GRIEF

"Grief is love with no place to go."

Dictionary.com defines grief as "keen mental suffering or distress over affliction or loss; sharp sorrow; painful regret." The American Psychological Association offers a similar definition: "the anguish experienced after significant loss, typically the death of a loved one." For those actively grieving, these definitions may feel cold and detached—at least, that's how they felt to me. The words that resonated most were 'distress,' 'sharp sorrow,' and 'anguish.' I know those feelings too well because I've lived them repeatedly. I've come to believe that grief is one of the most misunderstood emotions, second only to love. And ironically, grief and love are inseparable. Here's my definition of grief: it is love with no place to go.

What Grief Is

Several years after Bryant's passing, I joined a faith-based grief recovery group called *GriefShare*. That decision became a lifeline. Through this program, I began to understand the many emotions I was experiencing and why they came in relentless waves. I highly recommend *GriefShare* to anyone navigating the loss of a loved one. According to *GriefShare*, grief is a natural and normal response to loss—especially the death of a loved one. It encompasses many emotional, physical, and even spiritual reactions. They emphasize that everyone's grief journey is unique and shaped by personal, cultural, and spiritual factors.

I found validation in how *GriefShare* explained the emotions tied to grief. The ones listed below represent just a tiny portion of what they highlight:

Sadness and Sorrow: An overwhelming sense of loss and longing for the person gone.

Shock and Disbelief: Struggling to accept the reality of the loss, especially in the early days.

Anger: Sometimes directed at God, oneself, or the circumstances surrounding the loss.

Guilt: A sense of responsibility for what happened or regret over things left unsaid.

Fear and Anxiety: Worry about the future, financial struggles, or the fear of forgetting a loved one.

Loneliness and Isolation: A profound emptiness, especially when others seem to have "moved on."

Relief (for caregivers): After witnessing long-term suffering, relief may come with guilt.

Numbness: Emotional detachment that serves as a defense mechanism.

Understanding that these emotions were part of the normal grieving process brought me an unexpected sense of comfort. For the first time, I realized I wasn't losing my mind, going crazy, or failing at grief. These feelings existed because my love was so deep that its absence felt unbearable.

"Grief took away the color in my life, leaving me in complete darkness."

What Grief Is Not

Understanding grief is just as important as recognizing what it isn't. Society often imposes unrealistic expectations on those who are grieving, unintentionally causing more harm than good. Grief is deeply personal—it's not the same for everyone and, indeed, not a one-size-fits-all experience.

Grief is not linear: It doesn't follow a set timeline. You don't simply "move on" or "get over it." Instead, you learn to live with it.

Grief is unpredictable: One day, you might feel okay; the next, you're entirely unraveled. A familiar smell, a song, or even a random memory can trigger an emotional wave without warning.

Grief is not weakness: Tears, anger, and moments of despair are not signs of failure but reflections of love and humanity.

Grief is not something to 'fix': Well-meaning advice and clichés often miss the mark because grief isn't a problem—it's a process.

In the early days of my grief, I received a flood of unsolicited advice—how to act, what to say, even how to feel. People expected me to follow a script that didn't fit my reality. But grief isn't a script; it's a roller coaster with unexpected twists and turns—sometimes leaving you breathless, other times leaving you completely adrift.

The Physical and Mental Toll of Grief

Grief doesn't just affect your emotions—it can disrupt your entire way of thinking and functioning. After Bryant passed, I experienced what some call "grief fog." My memory became unreliable, and even the simplest tasks felt impossible. I still struggle with this.

Physically, I couldn't eat without feeling nauseous. I lost weight and was constantly fatigued. Sometimes, I couldn't manage basic tasks like brushing my teeth, combing my hair, or showering. Getting dressed felt out of the question. The most minor aches and pains triggered fears of serious illness—a byproduct of watching both my mom and Bryant succumb to cancer.

Isolation became my refuge. It was easier to be alone than to face the world's judgment or endure well-meaning dismissals of my pain. Grief drained the color from my life, leaving me in complete darkness.

Grief is Love That Endures

In the end, grief is love transformed. It's the continuation of a relationship that death cannot end. While the pain of loss never entirely disappears, neither does the love that gives it meaning.

GriefShare taught me that even in the darkest moments, there is hope. It doesn't come quickly or easily, but it's there. The pain isn't erased, but the Bible became my foundation when everything else felt unsteady. Grief isn't about forgetting—it's about remembering with tenderness, even as you learn to carry the weight of loss.

A Word of Encouragement

If you are grieving, know this: your journey is your own, and there is no right or wrong way to walk through it. Allow yourself the space to feel, mourn, question, and, in time, heal. Grief is not a burden to hide—it's evidence of a deep love that refuses to fade. And that kind of love will always find a way to endure.

Chapter 8
THE WEIGHT OF GUILT & REGRET IN GRIEF

"God's mercy fills in the gaps where I fell short."

After Bryant died, I was overwhelmed with guilt and regret. I found myself crying out loud to him, apologizing for his suffering and wishing I could have taken his place. I replayed every decision and every moment of his fight, questioning whether I had done enough.

As a mother, the instinct to "fix" things for your child is automatic. But when something as relentless as cancer invades, it renders you powerless in an almost unbearable way. No love or determination could have healed Bryant—yet I still struggled to accept that truth.

It has taken me nearly eight years to accept that I did everything I could for Bryant. But that journey was far from easy. One of the hardest lessons I learned is that parents must advocate fiercely for their children, especially in medical crises.

The Echoes of Guilt

Early on, I believed doctors always had the answers, but I quickly learned the value of second, third, and even fourth opinions. While Bryant was blessed with excellent doctors, they were only human. God is the ultimate physician, and only He holds the power over life and death.

Bryant understood this better than I did. From the beginning, he told me more times than I can count, "Mom, only God can number my days." His faith was unwavering, even as mine wavered under doubt.

I carried that doubt and guilt for a long time, replaying prayers I thought I should have prayed more fervently or differently. It felt like a weight I couldn't put down. But in His goodness, God reminded me that He saw my tears, my heart, and my love for Bryant. He gently helped me understand that I had done my best with what I knew then.

Regrets That Reach Back

Yet my regret ran deeper than Bryant's illness. It stretched back to my pregnancy with him, his birth, and his early years. At the time, my marriage was fractured by deception, leaving me to navigate a high-risk pregnancy alone. My focus was divided between managing my health, holding together a relationship that barely existed, and caring for a four-year-old.

Shortly after Bryant's birth, I became severely ill due to the betrayal I had endured and required intensive treatment to recover. We lived out of state, more than five hours from family and friends. My doctor wanted to admit me to the hospital, and in hindsight, I should have agreed. But because of the situation at home, I refused, settling instead for home health care and an IV in my arm for a month. That decision left some of my care—including administering medication through my IV—to my then-husband, the very person responsible for my suffering.

Those early months of Bryant's life were marked by emotional and physical hardship, leaving me with the haunting feeling that I had failed him long before his diagnosis.

As I worked to rebuild my life in the years that followed, the pain from those past struggles shaped the way I parented. And when Bryant passed, the weight of that unresolved hurt made my grief even heavier.

One of my dad's sermons stood out: **"Why Guilt is a Gift."** It felt as if he had thrown me a life raft. In that sermon, he reminded his congregation that guilt, though painful, can serve a greater purpose in our lives.

He explained that the Bible reveals four shadows of guilt through different stories:

Blaming Others (Adam) – Like Adam blamed Eve, we often deflect our guilt onto others to avoid responsibility. My ex blamed me for all of our problems. I wasn't without fault, but he never took responsibility for his part. At the same time, I blamed myself for Bryant's illness, as though I could have somehow prevented it.

Hidden in Kindness (Jacob) – Guilt can masquerade as acts of over-compensation, compelling us to "fix" what's broken—even when it's beyond our control.

Confusion About Roles (Mary and Martha) – Sometimes, guilt arises from misunderstanding our role—feeling like we should have done more or been more.

Denial and Regret (Peter) – As Peter denied Jesus, we may struggle to face our guilt, especially when it resurfaces unexpectedly in grief.

God's Purpose for Guilt

My dad also laid out four key truths about guilt—truths I held onto as I walked through my grief:

Guilt is a Gift for Growth

God uses guilt to point us toward repentance and restoration, not condemnation.

Fake Guilt is Dangerous

Many suffer from false guilt—judgments imposed by others or unrealistic expectations. But God's conviction is gentle, leading to healing rather than shame.

True Guilt Leads to Grace

Genuine guilt comes from God's Spirit, drawing us closer to Him through humility and dependence.

God Provides Forgiveness

1 John 1:9 reminds us, *"If we confess our sins, He is faithful and just to forgive us our sins and to cleanse us from all unrighteousness."*

My dad concluded the sermon with a powerful reminder: *"Trials can make us bitter or better. Don't let guilt weigh you down—let it drive you closer to the cross."*

Letting Go of Guilt

Over time, God softened the sharp edges of my guilt. I began to see it not as a punishment but as a reflection of how deeply I loved Bryant. My regrets weren't failures—they were proof of a mother's longing for more time, answers, and chances to show love.

Bryant's unwavering faith—his confidence in God's plan—became my example. He reminded me that even in my weakness, God's grace was sufficient (2 Corinthians 12:9).

Letting go of guilt didn't happen overnight. It took prayer, counseling, and, ultimately, surrendering my pain to God. Though I still have moments of doubt, I lean into the promise that where I fell short, God's mercy fills the gaps.

A Word for Those Struggling with Guilt

I see you—the mother who lies awake at night, questioning whether you did enough. I understand the ache of wishing for do-overs and the weight of *if only*.

But let me remind you: God's grace is greater than your guilt. He sees the silent tears you've cried. He hears the prayers too heavy for words. He knows your heart and doesn't measure you by mistakes, but by the love, you pour out.

Let guilt be a guide—not into despair, but into the arms of God, where forgiveness, grace, and healing await.

Your Child's Story Continues

Your child's story doesn't end with guilt—it lives on in the love you carry and the memories you cherish. Grief and guilt may walk beside you, but they don't have to define you.

Give yourself grace. You did enough. And where you fell short, God's mercy fills the gaps.

As Bryant taught me, there is peace in trusting that God's plan is always bigger than ours—even when we don't understand it.

Chapter 9
THE ISOLATION OF GRIEF

"...were they afraid my grief might somehow seep into their lives?"

The moment Bryant was diagnosed with cancer, both of our lives were upended. From that point on, we began to experience the isolation and fear that often accompany a terminal illness.

Bryant's chemotherapy treatments required hospitalization twice a month. The severity of the side effects meant we spent most of his two-year battle in the hospital. If we were lucky, we would have had a few days at home between stays, but those days were far from restful. Our "new normal," as we called it, revolved entirely around the hospital and the relentless treatment cycles.

The hospital became our home, and the world outside its walls faded. Life as we knew it before Bryant's diagnosis was over. Inside those walls, we formed a small community with other families fighting similar battles, but we could no longer relate to what was happening in the "normal" world beyond.

A Shrinking Circle

As Bryant's illness progressed, our social circle shrank. Friends I once thought would always be there began to disappear. It wasn't intentional, I'm sure, but we became less relatable to others.

Bryant was fiercely loved and well-known for his contagious smile, but he still had a core group of friends who stood by him for much of his journey. Yet, as his condition worsened, even he began to pull away. He didn't want his friends to see him in his weakened state. The pain he endured often made it impossible for him to tolerate visitors.

The Fear of Contagion

Even before Bryant passed, I could sense that people were fearful—not of Bryant himself, but of what his illness represented. Cancer became a stark reminder of life's fragility, particularly in someone so young and full of life.

After his death, I experienced this fear even more acutely. I'll never forget one of my first trips to the grocery store. I saw a friend I had known for more than 20 years. Our kids had grown up together, played sports together, and even had sleepovers. She wasn't a best friend, but we'd always been cordial.

When we met across the aisle, I smiled, but before I could speak, she turned and disappeared. I don't know if she left the store or purposely avoided me, but the rejection stung deeply. This wasn't an isolated incident—it happened again and again.

Was it because they didn't know what to say? Or were they afraid my grief might somehow seep into their own lives? I'll never truly know, but I began to understand over time. My loss had become a symbol of life's uncertainty and pain. For some, looking away was easier than confronting that vulnerability.

The Loneliness of Grief

This kind of isolation compounds the loneliness of grief. Not only had I lost my son, but I also felt as though I'd lost my place in the world. The life I once knew, the friendships I once cherished, were gone.

Grief makes you feel like an outsider. You walk through life as though you're invisible, as though your pain marks you as someone others don't want to get too close to. At first, it was difficult not to take it personally. I wanted to scream, "I haven't changed! I'm still me!" But the truth is, I had changed. Grief transformed me in ways others couldn't see or understand.

And yet, some people stayed.

The Courage to Stay

For those who remained by my side—who walked with Bryant and me through the fire and continued to speak his name after his passing—I will forever be grateful. They were few, but they didn't let fear or discomfort stop them from showing up.

Theresa Hanks, one of my dearest long-time friends, is one of the most selfless and loving people I know. She stood by Bryant and me every step of the way. When Bryant started seeing a doctor in New Orleans, she drove us to every appointment. She even took notes during consultations when my mind was too overwhelmed to process the details. She became my lifeline, bridging the gap between the isolating world of cancer and the world beyond.

Several days after Bryant's funeral, Theresa called to check on me.

At the time, I was alone at home. Everyone had returned to their everyday lives. I was drowning in grief so intense that I couldn't form coherent words. She was at my door within an hour, packing my bag to take me to her house. I stayed with her and her husband, **Steve**, for nearly a month. During that time, they made me a part of their lives. They fed me, loved me, and ensured I got out of bed and dressed each day. They even included me in their large family get-togethers. Then Christmas Day came.

It was Bryant's one-month anniversary of dying. I was going to the cemetery when I fell down the stairs and was taken from their home in an ambulance with a broken leg. On Christmas Day, Theresa left her family to sit with me in the ER without me even asking. Eight years later, I'm still invited to Theresa and Steve's family gatherings.

Their love saved me. Without it, I wouldn't be here today to share this story.

Grief Is Not Contagious

If you're grieving, please know this: your grief is not something to be afraid of. You are not contagious.

For those supporting someone in grief, remember that avoidance only deepens the isolation. You don't need the right words; you need to show up. Be willing to sit in the discomfort, to listen without judgment, and to walk through the pain together. It will be challenging, but it will also be healing.

Grief doesn't need to be silenced or avoided. It needs to be shared. In those moments of connection—when we truly allow ourselves to see and support one another—we find the compassion and strength to carry on.

A Final Word to Those Who Stay

To those who stand beside anyone grieving, your presence means more than you'll ever know. You are the anchor that keeps us grounded when the waves threaten to drown us. Whether you offer a shoulder to cry on, a meal to nourish us, or simply a listening ear, your support is an act of love that cannot be measured.

Theresa never left our side in Bryant's cancer fight. Driving us to his oncologist appointments in New Orleans was just one of the many ways she stood with us. These pictures were taken on two of those trips. Austin and Bryant never knew life without Theresa. They considered her a bonus mom.

WHAT EVERY GRIEVING MOTHER WISHES YOU KNEW

PART TWO

WRESTLING WITH GRIEF AND FAITH

Chapter 10
WHAT NOT TO SAY

"Grief is already heavy, and the wrong words can add to that weight."

When someone we love dies, people often struggle with what to say. They want to be helpful and offer comfort, but sometimes, their words unintentionally cause more harm than good. After Bryant died, I experienced firsthand how painful specific comments could be—even from well-meaning people.

Grief is already an immense burden, and the wrong words can make it even heavier. I've had people say things that left me stunned, hurt, and even angry. At times, their words deepened my sense of isolation, making me feel as if no one could understand what I was going through—and often, they didn't.

I'm sharing this chapter not to shame but to help people understand the effects of words. Most people don't intend to hurt grieving parents or loved ones, but our culture doesn't do a great job of teaching us how to respond to loss. I hope to help others better support grieving people by shedding light on what not to say.

You might assume that after living with loss since I was 12, I would know the right thing to say. But even now, there are moments when I struggle because grief isn't a one-size-fits-all experience. No two people grieve the same way. It's deeply personal, shaped by the individual, their loved one, and their unique bond.

Three months after my niece, Reagan, passed away, a woman at church asked how my brother and his wife were coping. I shared how they were doing, expecting words of kindness or compassion. Instead, she frowned, *"You mean they aren't over that already?"*

I was stunned. This was a godly woman I admired—someone who actively served in the church. Her lack of understanding felt like a slap in the face.

Years after Travis was killed in Afghanistan by an Afghan sniper, his mom, Beckie, kept his memory alive—much like I do on Facebook. One day, someone hiding behind a screen and keyboard left a cruel comment on one of her posts: *"Stop living in the past for Travis."*

I can only assume this person was never held and nurtured as an infant to be so heartless—to say something so callous to a grieving mother. I wouldn't wish such a profound loss on anyone, but if this person ever experiences the death of a child, it will shatter them. Completely. Only then will they understand the impact of their words.

A fellow cancer mom I met in the hospital, **Connie Lee**, faced an equally shocking moment in a grief support group after losing her 16-year-old son, **Johann Doum**. An older woman turned to Connie, asking, *"Does losing a son hurt as much as losing a husband?"*

Let me tell you—there is no comparison to losing a child. Not to diminish anyone's grief, but the truth is a child cannot be replaced like a husband can in some cases. I don't mean that to be disrespectful, as many widowers do remarry. Granted, many couples never have children, so losing a lifelong spouse for them is horrendous. And then there are older couples who have children, but those children have moved away and have lives they're no longer included in. For them, losing a spouse is a tremendous loss.

The worst comment I've ever heard wasn't even directed at me. It was said to Connie's daughter, **Delaney Doum**, just 11 years old when her brother Johann died. A church youth volunteer told her that her family must be under a *generational curse* because her brother died of cancer.

Words can cut like knives—especially when spoken to someone already carrying the unbearable weight of loss. Yes, there are passages in the Bible that reference the ripple effects of sin, suggesting that the actions of one generation can impact the next. But they also emphasize God's mercy and love toward those faithful. Jesus freed us on the cross.

To say something like that to a grieving child is beyond absurd.

I've faced similar comments. People told me, "He's in a better place," or "God needed another angel." Some condemned me for my anger toward God, questioning my faith and insisting, *"You can't question God."* But perhaps the most common phrase I heard was, *"God doesn't give you more than you can handle."*

While well-meaning, these words only deepened my heartache. But nothing compared to what my friends have endured.

Losing a child—whether to a long-term illness or an unexpected tragedy—is an indescribable grief. Even the most well-intended words can wound more than they comfort. But with understanding and thoughtfulness, we can all learn to offer support in ways that genuinely help grieving parents.

For me, writing these words comes easier than saying them. Based on my experience, here are ten examples of what not to say, why they can hurt, and better ways to offer support.

"Sometimes, the best thing you can do is say nothing."

1. "At least you had time to prepare."

No amount of time can prepare a parent for the loss of their child. The anticipatory grief I experienced during Bryant's 25-month battle with cancer did nothing to lessen the devastation of his death. This comment dismissed not only the agony of his illness but also the unbearable loss I carried alone.

Consider saying instead:
"I can't imagine how difficult this must be for you."

2. "He's in a better place."

Even for parents who believe in Heaven, this phrase minimizes the profound ache of missing their child.

My heart longed for Bryant to be here with me, not somewhere else—even if that somewhere was Heaven.

Consider saying instead:
"I know you miss him, and I'm here for you."

3. "At least he's no longer suffering."

While it's true that Bryant's suffering ended, my longing for him never did. This phrase, though well-intended, can feel dismissive of a parent's ongoing pain and yearning.

Consider saying instead:
"I'm so sorry for the pain you both went through."

4. "You can always have another child."

Children are not replaceable. This comment diminishes the unique and irreplaceable bond between a parent and the child they have lost.

Consider saying instead:
"Bryant was so special. I'm here to remember him with you."

5. "At least you have other children (or family)."

The presence of other loved ones does not lessen the pain of losing a child. This phrase can make grieving parents feel they are expected to "move on" or focus on gratitude rather than mourning.

For those who are grieving, remember this—you are not a burden. Your pain is not something to be apologized for; it is a reflection of love. Surround yourself with people who are unafraid of your tears. And when others turn away, trust that God will always remain. You are not alone in your grief. Even in the depths of isolation, there is hope.

Consider saying instead:
"Your love for Bryant was extraordinary. I know your heart aches for him."

6. "It's time to move on."

Grief has no timeline. Comments like this invalidate a parent's mourning and place unnecessary pressure on them to "heal" on someone else's schedule.

Consider saying instead:
"I'll walk alongside you for as long as it takes."

7. "I know exactly how you feel."

Even if someone has experienced a similar loss, grief is profoundly personal and unique. Comparisons—especially those involving pets—can unintentionally shift the focus away from the grieving parent and minimize their pain.

Consider saying instead:
"I can't imagine your pain, but I want to support you however I can."
or
"I'm here to listen if you want to share your feelings."

8. "You're so strong."

Though well-intentioned, this phrase can add pressure to "hold it together" when grieving parents are barely surviving. Strength is often a necessity, not a choice.

Consider saying instead:
"It's okay to feel broken. I'm here to support you however you need."
or
"You don't have to be strong. It's okay to cry and fall apart. I'll be here to help pick up the pieces."

9. "Everything happens for a reason."

This is one of the most common phrases spoken after a tragedy—and one of the most hurtful. I've heard it more times than I can count, making me want to scream each time.

To a grieving parent, this phrase can feel dismissive. It suggests that there was some grand, divine reason for their child's death as if any reason could justify their pain.

I wrestled with my faith after Bryant died. In my darkest moments, I questioned everything. But I could never believe that God "needed" my son more than I did. This thinking reduces grief to a shallow explanation that does nothing to bring comfort—it only raises more questions.

10. "God will never give you more than you can handle."

This one stung every time I heard it. People often quote it as scripture, but it misinterprets **1 Corinthians 10:13**, which speaks about resisting temptation—not enduring suffering.

The truth is, my son's death *was* more than I could handle. It shattered me in ways I never thought possible. There were days I didn't think I'd survive, let alone find the strength to get out of bed.

The weight of grief is overwhelming. Hearing this phrase made me feel like I wasn't strong or faithful enough because I *couldn't* handle it.

A better response might be:
"I can't imagine how hard this is, but I'm here for you."
or
"I don't have answers, but I love you and will walk with you through this."

When Silence Is Better Than Words

Sometimes, the best thing you can do is say nothing at all. Grieving parents don't always need answers—they need presence. A hug, a hand to hold, or simply sitting silently can speak volumes.

I eventually learned that we aren't meant to carry grief alone. God doesn't expect us to shoulder its weight alone. Instead, He meets us in our weakness and carries us through.

A Final Thought for Those Supporting the Grieving

Grief is messy, unpredictable, and deeply personal. No words can erase the pain of loss, but there are ways to make the journey less lonely.

Don't feel pressured to have the perfect words if you're supporting someone grieving. Focus on showing up, listening, and being present. And if you're suffering, and someone says the wrong thing, allow yourself to feel hurt—but also know that their intentions are likely good, even if their words fall short.

Above all, remember this: grief is a reflection of love. It's not something to fix or rush through. It's something to *honor*. Offering compassion, patience, and grace is always the best response.

Chapter 11
PLEASE SAY THEIR NAME

"The truth is, not hearing his name hurts far more than hearing it."

One of the most painful things I've experienced since losing Bryant is the silence—so few people still say his name. It started the moment he died, as if his last breath erased him from existence for everyone but me.

In their minds, Bryant was gone. And in a physical sense, I understand that. But he's still very much alive in my heart. His earthly body may no longer be here, but I see him in my dreams, in our memories, and in the love we shared. My love for him didn't die with his body—if anything, it has only grown stronger. I will never stop loving Bryant. It's simply not possible.

But when people don't say his name, it feels like his life, dreams, and all the memories we made together are being erased. Bryant's story didn't end when he died—it lives on through the people who knew him, loved him, and were inspired by him.

The Pain of Silence

I can't count the times I've encountered someone I once knew well who avoids mentioning Bryant altogether. It's almost as if they're afraid that saying his name will somehow remind me that he's gone—as if I could ever forget.

The truth is, not hearing his name hurts far more than hearing it. The silence is deafening, like a wall separating me from a world that keeps moving forward while I remain frozen.

I've had people turn and walk away in public to avoid me. Others seem uncomfortable when I mention Bryant as if bringing him up is a breach of etiquette. But there is no etiquette manual for grief. No rulebook dictates how long it's "appropriate" to keep someone's memory alive. For a parent, that time is forever.

Sometimes, people avoid saying his name because they don't want to "make me cry." What they don't realize is that I'm already crying—inside, if not outwardly—because I miss him so much. Saying his name doesn't bring pain. It brings comfort. It brings connection. It reminds me that he mattered—not just to me, but to others.

Why It Matters to Say Their Name

Bryant's life was nothing short of spectacular. He was an old soul with a heart bigger than Texas, a smile framed by the prettiest dimples, and an unmatched love for people. He never met a stranger, and his kindness was imprinted on everyone he met.

Years after his passing, I still hear stories about Bryant—stories I had never heard. People tell me how he encouraged them during hard times, how his smile brightened their day, or how he made them feel seen and loved.

Whenever someone shares one of these stories, they give me a precious gift. It reassures me that Bryant's life made a difference, and his memory hasn't faded.

Saying Bryant's name honors his memory and keeps his legacy alive. When his name goes unspoken, I fear he'll be forgotten, which terrifies me.

Memories That Breathe Life

"... their names hold power -the power to heal, remember, and love without end."

When someone does say Bryant's name, it's like music to my ears. One friend recently said, "I was thinking about Bryant today." Another shared a memory of a late-night trip to Waffle House that reminded them of him. Those simple acknowledgments mean the world to me.

I can't fully describe how comforting it is that Bryant still crosses people's minds. It reassures me that his life mattered, and his absence hasn't erased the impact he made.

Practical Ways to Keep Their Name Alive

For those who may not know what to say to someone grieving, here are a few suggestions that can make a big difference:

"I was thinking about Bryant today and smiled."

"I saw something that reminded me of Bryant and had to tell you."

"I miss Bryant too."

"I'll never forget how Bryant brightened every room he walked into."

"I'd love to hear a story about Bryant if you'd like to share it."

Sharing memories keeps their story alive. Whether it's a funny story, a touching moment, or something simple, these reminders let grieving parents know their child isn't forgotten.

A Mother's Greatest Fear

One of my greatest fears is that Bryant will be forgotten. I never want to lose the sound of his laugh, the sparkle in his eyes, or the warmth of his hugs. I want people to remember him for the incredible person he was—the joy he brought and the kindness he showed.

When someone says his name, it keeps his memory alive. It reminds me that his story isn't over—it's still being written in the lives he touched.

Grieving parents don't need their child's name erased from the conversation—they need it spoken with love, courage, and remembrance. It reminds us that their story isn't finished—it's still being told in every word, every memory, and every heart that dares to speak their name.

Say Their Name—Always

So, say their name. Say her name. Speak it with love, share it with laughter, whisper it in prayer. Let the names of the ones we've lost remain part of our conversations, stories, and lives. Because even in the silence of their absence, their names hold power—the power to heal, to remember, and to love without end.

To the grieving mother who fears her child will be forgotten, know this: their story is far from over. Each time their name is spoken, it's a reminder that love never dies—it lives on through the memories we keep and the voices that refuse to let them fade. Bryant's name will always be on my lips, and I hope it will always be on yours, too.

"I have you in my heart." — *Philippians 1:7 (NIV)*

Chapter 12
WHEN FAITH FEELS FRAGILE

"Prayer isn't about controlling the outcome but surrendering it."

Grief shakes the foundation of everything we once believed true—especially our faith. After Bryant's diagnosis, I found myself leaning on God like never before, praying fervently for healing and clinging to every scripture of hope I could find. But as his condition worsened, my prayers became more challenging to speak, and my faith felt more fragile than ever.

I've always believed in the power of prayer. I was raised to trust God's plan and believe He works all things together for good. But what happens when that belief is tested—when the answers you pray for don't come?

Every second of Bryant's fight was consumed with uncertainty. His care plan evolved so rapidly that I could hardly comprehend it all. The barrage of medical information, decisions, and setbacks overwhelmed me. In those moments, prayer felt impossible. It wasn't for a lack of faith; I didn't have the words. I often felt disconnected from God during Bryant's illness. I doubted my ability to pray and sometimes even questioned God's presence.

The Struggle to Pray

When Bryant was fighting cancer, I often felt like I wasn't praying enough. It wasn't that I didn't want to—I didn't know how. I was emotionally and spiritually drained, too exhausted to form the right words. I remember nights in the hospital when I would sit beside his bed and cry, unable to do anything but whisper, "God, please."

There were moments when my prayers fell silent. I wondered if God was listening, and if He was, why wasn't He answering? I desperately wanted miracles but felt like I was met with silence instead.

One Sunday, more than 324 churches across the country held a special time of intercessory prayer for Bryant. While their faith was inspiring, it also left me feeling inadequate. Why couldn't I pray like that? Why did my faith feel so weak in comparison?

Guilt began to creep in. Was I failing Bryant by not praying hard enough? Did my doubt somehow stand in the way of his healing?

Silent Cries and Surrender

As Bryant's illness progressed, my prayers began to change. I stopped begging for a miracle and started praying for peace—for him, me, and our family. I didn't have the words to pray eloquently, so I offered God my silence, trusting that He could hear the cries of my heart, even when I couldn't speak them aloud.

One of the most profound moments of surrender came when Bryant told me he wasn't afraid to die. His faith remained strong, even as his body grew weaker. He spoke of heaven with a peace that both comforted and broke me. I didn't understand it then, but I do now—Bryant's faith carried him in ways mine couldn't. And in time, his peace began to hold me, too.

The Weight of Promising Prayer

After Bryant's death, people often said, "I'm praying for you." While I appreciated their intentions, I sometimes wondered if they meant it or were struggling to find the words, just like I had.

Even now, I hesitate to promise someone I'll pray for them unless I know I can follow through. I understand how sacred those words are, and I know what it feels like to lean on the prayers of others when your faith feels too fragile to stand.

When Worship Feels Like Prayer

In the months following Bryant's passing, I found solace not in spoken prayers but in music. I would sit in the dark, letting hymns wash over me—songs like *It Is Well With My Soul* and *Great Is Thy Faithfulness*. Each note reminded me of God's promises, filling the spaces where my words failed. In those quiet moments, the music became my prayers, speaking for me when I couldn't find the strength.

WHAT EVERY GRIEVING MOTHER WISHES YOU KNEW

The Silent Cry

Many days, my prayers were nothing more than a desperate whisper: *God, please help me. I can't do this alone.* Those words often slipped out between sobs so raw and deep that I could barely breathe. The silence that followed felt more honest than any spoken plea ever could.

Late at night, after the world had gone still, I would sit in Bryant's hospital room, watching him sleep. I would count his breaths, the rise and fall of his chest anchoring me to the present while silent tears traced paths down my cheeks. In those moments, I clung to the belief that God understood the prayers my heart could not shape into words.

I found comfort in Romans 8:26: *"The Spirit himself intercedes for us through wordless groans."* That verse reminded me that even in my silence, God was listening and speaking on my behalf when I no longer knew how to pray.

A Shift Toward Surrender

Bryant's faith never wavered. He often spoke to me about his acceptance of death, describing the profound peace he felt in knowing he would be healed in heaven. His words were a testament to his strength, yet they were also painful to hear. But in those moments, I saw God's presence reflected in Bryant's unwavering trust.

One of the most profound lessons I learned during that time was that prayer isn't about controlling the outcome but surrendering it. Letting go doesn't mean giving up; it means trusting that God's plan is greater than anything we can comprehend.

Finding Prayer in Presence

With time, I came to understand that prayer isn't always spoken. It doesn't need to be eloquent or even voiced aloud. Sitting in silence, holding Bryant's hand, or simply resting in God's presence—those moments were prayers, too.

I've learned that prayer is as much about presence as it is about words. It's about opening your heart, even when it feels shattered, and trusting that God hears you. When you struggle to pray, lean into the prayers of others. Let their faith carry you when yours feels weak. And if even that feels out of reach, take comfort in knowing that God is still near.

He meets you in your pain, exactly as you are—not as you think you should be. You don't need to have all the answers or even the strength to form the questions. Prayer isn't about perfection; it's about connection. God knows your heart whether you sit silently, cry in desperation, or whisper the faintest plea for peace.

Remember, prayer isn't just about asking in times of doubt—it's about trusting. Sometimes, the most powerful prayer is simply showing up, as broken and weary as you are, and allowing God to hold you.

Practical Tools for Prayer When Words Fail

If you're struggling to pray, here are a few practices that helped me reconnect with God, even in my darkest moments:

- **Scripture Prayers** – When I didn't know what to say, I let God's Word speak for me. Many songs on YouTube and other online platforms use actual Scripture set to music, allowing me to pray through song.

- **Worship Through Music** – When words failed me, music gave them back. Hymns I grew up singing, and contemporary songs became my prayers.

- **Journaling** – Writing to God helped me process emotions I couldn't verbalize. My journal became a sacred space to release anger, ask questions, and express gratitude.

- **Breath Prayers** – Short, simple prayers like *"Jesus, help me"* were all I could manage some days. And that was enough.

A Quiet Hope

Over time, my understanding of prayer has deepened. In the depths of my grief, I doubted God's presence. But looking back now, I see He was always with me—going before me, making a way, even when I couldn't recognize it.

Today, my prayers are no longer silent. If anything, they are constant. I talk to God about everything and often joke that He probably misses the quieter moments we used to share.

An Offering to Those Struggling with Prayer

If you are struggling with prayer, I want you to know this: God hears you, even in the silence. Your prayers don't have to be perfect and don't always require words. Sometimes, the most straightforward *help me* carries more weight than the most eloquent plea.

Daphne Luchsinger visits with Bryant in the hospital. She was Austin's kindergarten teacher. Bryant was only 9 months old and quickly became the class mascot. Daphne was instrumental in getting Bryant on Immunotherapy.

Ken and Melissa Jernigan were such a blessing to us and Kena's family. They hosted us at their restaurant several times and held a benefit for us.

Chapter 13
FROM FAITH TO FURY

"I never imagined I could feel such overwhelming fury toward God."

Emotions like anger and sadness are part of being human, and God created us with these feelings for a reason. So, it shouldn't be surprising that anger is deeply woven into grief. Within the first three months after my son died, anger consumed me. I fought against it, but in my despair, I wasn't strong enough to withstand it. I never imagined I could feel such overwhelming fury toward God.

I was raised to believe you should never question God and accept whatever He gives you without resistance. But this loss shattered everything I thought I knew. The anger came faster, easier, and fiercer than I had anticipated.

Worse still, I found myself questioning God even as my anger raged. I desperately wanted to know why He had allowed Bryant to suffer the way he did. Bryant was a remarkable person. Why him? Of all people, why was he the one to endure such brutal, undeserved pain?

When the Questions Won't Stop

Why did God allow this to happen? Why didn't He stop it? I knew He could prevent it, so why didn't He? These questions spun in my mind, leaving me reeling as I struggled to understand everything.

The Weight of Judgment

When I voiced my anger, I was met with chastisement. People—often well-meaning—offered their opinions freely, even when I hadn't asked. Their words only deepened my bitterness, like salt rubbed into an open wound.

Biblical Examples of Honest Questions

My questions weren't born from defiance but love—love for Bryant, confusion about his suffering, and a desperate need to understand God's plan. Even Job cried out to God in his suffering, and Jesus himself questioned God while hanging on the cross. If they could bring their raw, honest pain before God, I could, too.

Job 3:11 says, *"Why did I not perish at birth and die as I came from the womb?"* And in Matthew 27:46, Jesus cried out, *"My God, my God, why have you forsaken me?"*

These scriptures let me wrestle with my pain and helped me realize that even the strongest in faith have asked God why.

The Turning Point

As I sat in my anger, drowning in frustration, one person did the unthinkable—something no one else had done. While others chastised me, **Linda Carden**, a friend of my mother's, called to check on me. She didn't offer advice or rebuke me for my emotions.

Instead, she let me speak freely—about Bryant, my sorrow, and the rage I could barely contain.

I didn't hold back. I told her how furious I was that God had chosen Bryant for this journey instead of one of the countless ungrateful boys I'd seen in the news—boys who lived recklessly, addicted to drugs, committing crimes—even murder.

I'll never forget her response. In a calm, steady voice filled with love, she said, *"Janet, have you ever thought that maybe those other boys weren't ready to go home? Bryant was."*

Her words hit me like a ton of bricks. Shame washed over me. How could I so quickly wish death upon another human being, especially someone who didn't know Jesus like Bryant did? The weight of my anger broke me.

Tears poured from me like a cleansing flood, washing away the bitterness that had taken root in my heart. And in that moment, something shifted. I never looked at Bryant's death the same way again.

Unlike other emotions in grief, anger never came back for a second or third round. For me, it was one and done. But that doesn't mean it will be the same for you—and that's okay.

God's Grace Through My Anger

My self-imposed anger only deepened my isolation in grief. I let bitterness take root in my heart, allowing it to settle there. Yet, the God I serve understood exactly where my anger and questions came from. He was patient with me, never turning away, never giving up.

God accepts us in our anger—He welcomes our honesty and vulnerability. More than anyone, He understands our pain and meets us where we are.

Scripture is filled with examples of faithful people wrestling with frustration and sorrow. In **Numbers 11:11–15**, Moses cried out in exasperation over leading the Israelites and their constant complaints. In **Lamentations 5:20**, Jeremiah pleaded, *"Why do you always forget us? Why do you forsake us so long?"* Even King David poured out his anger and sorrow in the Psalms.

These verses reminded me that God isn't afraid of my emotions. He's big enough to handle my anger and loving enough to lead me through it.

Practical Steps for Processing Anger Toward God

"God isn't afraid of my emotions—He's big enough to handle my anger and loving enough to lead me through it."

Grief needs space to breathe.

Suppressing anger doesn't make it disappear—it only buries it deeper. I allowed myself to feel and express those emotions, trusting that God could handle them. Journaling became a safe outlet, allowing me to release the turmoil inside.

Seek God in the Questions

Instead of pulling away from God, I ran toward Him—even when my words were raw and laced with anger. I poured out my heart, trusting that He would listen. Talking to trusted friends who shared my faith also helped me see His love more clearly through scripture.

Release Control

I had to accept that I might never get the answers I longed for this side of Heaven. Surrendering that need was difficult, but I leaned into Isaiah 55:8–9, which reminds us:

"For my thoughts are not your thoughts, neither are your ways my ways, declares the Lord."

That verse became a lifeline, reminding me to trust **God's plan—even when I couldn't understand it.**

Finding Hope After the Anger

By God's grace, peace found me after I laid my anger at His feet. I felt His presence again, steady and unwavering. Psalm 73:26 became my anchor:

"My flesh and my heart may fail, but God is the strength of my heart and my portion forever."

Even when my faith felt fragile, His love remained constant.

An Invitation to Trust Again

If you are angry with God, know this: **He understands.** He sees your pain, hears your questions, and welcomes you exactly as you are—raw, broken, and searching.

It's okay to cry out to Him. It's okay to admit you're angry. The God who created you also created your emotions, and He isn't afraid of them.

Take time to sit with your feelings and bring them before Him. Lean into the promise of **Romans 8:38–39.**

"For I am convinced that neither death nor life, neither angels nor demons, neither the present nor the future, nor any powers… will be able to separate us from the love of God."

Nothing—not your anger, questions, or doubts—can separate you from His love. His grace is big enough to handle your hardest questions, and His mercy is strong enough to carry you through your deepest struggles.

Trust Him. Even in your pain, He is holding you and leading you toward peace.

Chapter 14
THE RIGHT TO GRIEVE PUBLICLY

"...grief isn't about making others comfortable.
It's about doing what you need to survive."

After Bryant passed, I found solace in sharing memories of him on social media. It wasn't just about keeping his memory alive—it was about reminding myself and others that his life **mattered.** He was more than his illness, more than the battle he fought, and more than the day he died. These posts weren't just for me; they were a way to honor him, express my love, and let the world see the profound impact he had on my life.

Turning to Social Media for Support

Before Bryant's cancer diagnosis, I didn't even have a Facebook page. My job at the newspaper already put me in the public eye, and I never felt the need for one.

But when Bryant got sick, the outpouring of love and concern from friends, family, and even strangers became overwhelming. My phone rang constantly, and text messages flooded in, asking for updates. No matter how much I wanted to respond to every message, it became impossible to keep up.

That's when someone suggested I create a Facebook page dedicated to Bryant's journey. In this space, I could keep everyone informed without the emotional and mental exhaustion of repeating the same information repeatedly. It was one of the best decisions I ever made.

But the page became more than just a way to share updates—it became a **lifeline.** It gave me a place to pour out my heart, share my fears, celebrate Bryant's victories, and grieve his setbacks. Looking back, I'm grateful that I documented so much of his journey. Today, those posts appear as memories on my timeline, allowing me to relive moments with him. While they often bring tears, they also bring **healing.**

Criticism and Judgment

Mostly, the responses to my posts about Bryant have been overwhelmingly positive. People often share how he inspired them, how they still think of him, and how his story touched their lives. Those words bring comfort, reminding me that his impact didn't fade with his passing.

But not everyone has been supportive.

I've faced criticism—hurtful comments telling me to "move on" or even suggesting I delete my posts. And the most painful part? These remarks didn't come from strangers, but from people, I knew. One, in particular, caught me off guard, their words cutting deeper than I expected. At that moment, it felt as if my grief was being dismissed—as if mourning my son in a way that made sense to me was somehow wrong.

These critics didn't understand that my posts weren't about being "stuck" or refusing to move forward. They were about **processing** my grief. Sharing memories of Bryant didn't trap me in the past; it became a lifeline in the present. It was my way of honoring him, of keeping his presence alive—not just for me, but for everyone who loved him.

The Pressure to Move On

Telling someone to "move on" suggests that grief has an endpoint, as if one day, we're supposed to wake up and be done with it. But the truth is, grief is lifelong. It changes shape and intensity, but it never disappears.

For grieving parents, especially, the idea of "moving on" can feel like a betrayal—like letting go of our sorrow means letting go of our child. But healing doesn't mean forgetting. It means finding ways to carry their memory forward while still choosing to live.

Sharing Bryant's story on social media was never about staying stuck in the past; it was about integrating my love for him into the present and future. It was about keeping his light shining, even in his absence.

The truth is that grief is deeply personal. Some people grieve in silence, while others—like me—grieve openly. Social media became my space to mourn, honor Bryant's life, and invite others to remember him with me.

However, I quickly learned that not everyone understands this need. Some saw my posts as oversharing; others found them inspiring. Grief isn't about making others comfortable. It's about doing what you need to survive.

Why I'll Always Share Bryant's Story

"This person mattered. Their life mattered. And I still need them to matter."

Even if it's twenty years from now, I'll still be sharing Bryant's story. Why? Because no one has the right to dictate how I grieve or how I remember my child. My memories are mine—sacred and untouchable.

Grief doesn't come with an expiration date, and neither does love. Bryant will always be my son, just as I will always be his mother. Just as I wouldn't stop talking about my living children, I will never stop talking about Bryant. His illness or his death did not define his life; it was shaped by his kindness, courage, and the love he shared with others. Keeping his legacy alive means sharing those memories.

Some people may forget him over time, but I never will. As his mother, I have the right to remember him in my way, and I will always defend that right.

Why Sharing Is Healing

Despite the criticism, I continue to share memories of Bryant because doing so keeps me connected to him, to the love we shared, and to others who loved him, too. Every post is an opportunity—to honor him, to let the world know his life mattered, and to remind others that they are not alone in their grief.

I've received countless messages from people thanking me for sharing my story. Some have said it helped them process their losses. Others have told me it encouraged them to speak about their loved ones and break the silence surrounding grief. Grief needs community, not silence.

A Call for Compassion

To anyone who struggles to understand why grieving parents share their loss publicly, I ask you to consider this: Those posts are not cries for attention; they are cries for connection. They are ways of saying, "This person mattered. Their life mattered. And I still need them to matter."

Rather than offering criticism, offer compassion. Instead of urging someone to "move on," simply sit with them in their grief. Acknowledge their loss. Say their loved one's name. Be a source of comfort, not judgment.

A Word of Encouragement

To those who grieve publicly   do not let anyone shame you into silence. You have every right to honor your loved one in whatever way comforts you. Whether through pictures, stories, or written reflections, your grief is yours to express.

And to those supporting someone who is grieving, remember that your presence matters far more than your advice. Grief does not disappear but becomes more bearable when we feel seen, heard, and supported. Whether your grief is public or private, know this—you are not alone. God sees your heart, and He will carry you through.

Chapter 15
PRACTICAL WAYS TO HELP

"Grief doesn't require perfect words—it involves companionship."

When a child battles a long-term illness, the community often rallies around the family, offering support and prayers. The loss is not just personal—it is shared by everyone who has followed the journey. That was true for us. Individuals and churches became deeply invested in Bryant's story, lifting us with prayers and unwavering support.

At the time of Bryant's diagnosis, I worked at the local newspaper, and news of his condition spread quickly. My absence from work and details of my son's illness became public knowledge. Thousands of readers who had followed my writing in the newspaper began following his fight against cancer. When I left my job to be with Bryant, I gave no thought to how I would manage financially. I never hesitated. First and foremost, I was a mother, and there was no way I was going to let my son face such a monster alone.

The Blessing of Community Support

People from our church and beyond rallied together, organizing fundraisers to help meet our financial needs. The community followed suit, launching car washes, t-shirt sales, bake sales, gift basket raffles, benefit dinners, and more. These generous efforts allowed me to focus on Bryant without worrying about unpaid bills.

While financial support was essential, our daily lives had come to a screeching halt. As a single mother, I felt overwhelmed by how our world had been uprooted. Thankfully, so many people wanted to help—but I often struggled to respond to their offers. In situations like ours, people genuinely want to support grieving families but usually hesitate, unsure of what to do, or fearful of overstepping. But, at the same time, such as in our situation, I was completely overwhelmed with new information, new treatments, new doctors, and the stressors of watching my son suffer every day, leaving me with the inability to think outside of those lines. I wanted my son healed, and it just wasn't possible to think of anything beyond that point.

The Power of Small Gestures

Through this experience, I learned that taking initiative is one of the most meaningful ways to help. Instead of saying, *"Let me know how I can help,"* step in and do what you know needs to be done. Trust me when I say you won't be chastised for such actions but praised and never forgotten for being such a blessing.

Early in Bryant's hospitalization, a friend, **Amanda Carnley DeGraff**, noticed my garbage cans were full as she passed by my house. She sent me a message asking if she could move them to the road for pickup. While it may seem small, it meant the world to me.

Another time, a large delivery box sat empty on my front porch. We weren't home to dispose of it, nor did we have the means. That same friend and her husband, **Tony**, took care of it for me, lifting one more burden off my shoulders.

Her mother, **Terri Carnley**, also stepped up without being asked. Knowing that Gatorade and certain foods were some of the only things Bryant could tolerate, she organized a community collection to ensure we had plenty. These acts of kindness may have seemed simple to them, but to me, they were profoundly helpful and reminders that we weren't alone.

Years later, this same family faced their own devastating battle when Tony was diagnosed with a brain tumor. Through surgery, chemotherapy, and radiation, God brought healing—but they will be the first to say that it was faith, community support, and countless prayers that carried them through.

In late March, a follow-up scan revealed a recurrence in the same spot as before, requiring a second brain surgery. The procedure was successful, but their journey is far from over, and they need our prayers. Cancer is relentless and unforgiving.

Their kindness to us wasn't just about what they did—it was about how they saw a need and took action without waiting to be asked. Those simple yet powerful acts of love and generosity made a lasting impact and will never be forgotten.

Practical Ways to Help

Household Assistance

Yard work: Mow the lawn, rake leaves, shovel snow, or water plants.

Cleaning: Tidy up, vacuum, dust, or deep-clean high-traffic areas.

Laundry: Wash, fold, and put away clothes.

Meal preparation: Organize meal trains, deliver freezer meals, or drop off simple snacks.

Pet care: Feed, walk, or groom the family's pets.

Errands and Logistics

Household Assistance

Grocery shopping: Pick up essentials like toiletries, medications, or pet food.

Mail sorting and organization: Help sift through mail, pay bills, and file essential papers. Brain fog is real, and during times of grief or stress, even the simplest tasks can feel overwhelming.

Vehicle maintenance: Wash the car, fill the gas tank, or arrange for an oil change.

Gift cards: Provide gift cards for gas, groceries, or restaurants to help ease financial burdens.

Emotional and Social Support: Sometimes, the most significant help comes simply from being there.

Be present: Sit in silence, offer a hug, or listen without feeling the need to provide solutions.

Help with communication: Act as a spokesperson to relay updates to others. Manage phone calls, texts, emails, or social media posts to lighten the emotional load.

Encourage outings: Invite them for a meal, coffee, or a walk to help break the isolation.

Assist with thank-you notes: Help write and send thank-you cards for the support they've received.

Long-Term and Holiday Support

Grief doesn't end with the funeral. Support is needed long after the initial loss.

Check in regularly. Grief resurfaces during anniversaries, birthdays, and holidays. A simple message or call can mean the world.

Offer holiday assistance: Help with decorating, planning, or simply sitting together to ease the weight of special occasions.

Encourage self-care: Gently suggest simple ways to rest and recharge, whether it's a quiet afternoon, a walk, or a small act of self-kindness.

Provide meals on difficult days: Prepare or deliver meals during anniversaries or moments when they may feel most alone.

Thoughtful Gestures

Send personal notes or cards: A simple, heartfelt message can leave a lasting impact.

Create keepsakes: Help assemble scrapbooks, memory jars, or ornaments to honor their loved ones.

Offer grief-related books: Share resources that provide comfort and guidance in healing.

The Gift of Presence

One of the most meaningful things you can do for someone who is grieving is to stay. In the weeks and months after a funeral, life moves forward for most people, but for a grieving parent, their world remains shattered. This is when your presence matters most. Even if you don't know what to say, show up anyway. Grief doesn't require perfect words—it involves companionship.

Simply having coffee together, sitting quietly on the porch, or sending a message that says, *"I'm thinking about you,"* can make all the difference.

There was a local woman we didn't know who made personalized cards on her computer and mailed them to us every week for 25 months—and even beyond. Sometimes, she would tuck in two sticks of Juicy Fruit spearmint gum. We looked forward to those cards, her heartfelt messages, and even the gum. The smallest gestures can mean the most.

Bryant wanted to meet her, but we were in the hospital more than at home and never had the chance. I hope she, or someone who knows her, is reading this. Because of her selfless act of love, she comforted our hearts and lifted our spirits countless times.

Then, the prayer cards randomly appeared in the mailbox from churches praying for Bryant. It is a great ministry and was very much appreciated by us both, but when the cards continued to come with a handwritten note saying they were praying for Bryant months and even years after he died, it hit in a complex, painful way. Prayer ministry such as that requires constant and accurate updates. Upon receiving those cards after Bryant died, I was left drowning in tears and heartbreak. It wasn't intended for harm, but it certainly inflicted pain.

A Call to Action

The courage to step up and take action, even in small ways, can make all the difference for someone in crisis. Your kindness will never be forgotten; it will leave a lasting impact on the hearts of those you help.

Grief is heavy, but no one should have to carry it alone. Whether it's a warm meal, a kind word, or simply showing up when others have disappeared—or even sending a stick of gum in the mail—your support becomes a vital part of their healing.

To those offering help: don't wait for permission—act compassionately. And to those grieving: know it's okay to lean on others and let them help carry the weight. Love moves us forward, even when the burden feels too heavy.

PART THREE

PAIN, PURPOSE, AND PEACE

Chapter 16
WHEN THE
HOLIDAYS HURT

"Grief doesn't take a holiday, and healing doesn't follow a calendar."

The holidays used to be my favorite time of year. Bryant loved them, too—especially Thanksgiving and Christmas. Thanksgiving was always a big deal in our house, not just because of the food and family time but also because it meant Black Friday shopping.

Bryant loved hunting with my brother for the best deals, weaving through the chaos in search of hidden treasures. I still smile, remembering the excitement they shared, the stories they brought back, and the traditions they built together.

But Thanksgiving is different now. Instead of being a day to celebrate, it marks the anniversary of Bryant's last days. The empty chair at the table isn't just a reminder that he's gone—it's a symbol of the void his absence has left.

The Weight of the Season

I used to decorate the house for fall and Christmas every year. Pumpkins, candles, wreaths, garlands—our home was always alive with the season's sights, smells, and colors. I looked forward to filling our space with warmth and joy.

But since Bryant died, the holidays have become more challenging to face. For some years, the desire to decorate is entirely overshadowed by the weight of grief.

This year, I didn't put up a tree. I didn't hang a wreath. I didn't set out the pumpkins or string the lights. And it's not the first time I've skipped decorating altogether. Sometimes, just the thought of pulling out the decorations feels too heavy. It's not just about the effort—it's about what those decorations represent.

They're reminders of what's missing. They highlight the memories we once made and the traditions Bryant loved. They make the absence louder, not quieter.

Birthdays Without Him—A New Tradition

Bryant's birthday has become another bittersweet milestone. I want to celebrate his life—to honor the day he was born and the joy he brought into the world. But it's also a day that reminds me of all the birthdays he'll never have.

Last year, we did something different. Austin, his wife, and their two little girls joined me to celebrate Bryant's birthday. I hope it began a new tradition that allows us to remember Bryant with love, laughter, and joy.

We started the day by visiting Bryant's grave. Austin's stepdaughters, too young to fully understand, asked endless questions about Bryant and why he was there. Their curiosity melted my heart, but what struck me most was the innocence and tenderness they showed. One of the girls knelt down and gently rubbed Bryant's picture on his headstone with her fingers as if she'd always known him.

From there, we went to one of Bryant's favorite steakhouses, where we had celebrated one of his birthdays years earlier with Austin and his friends. Sitting there, eating dinner, and reminiscing was bittersweet. I could almost see Bryant laughing at that table, soaking in the moment, just as he had all those years ago.

We ended the night at a cupcake shop, a quiet nod to Bryant's tradition of bringing cupcakes to the hospital nurses during his treatments. That small gesture was the perfect tribute to his kindness—one final way to honor his generous spirit.

Guilt Over Skipping Traditions

"It's painful to realize the world has moved on while your grief still feels as raw as ever."

I've carried guilt for not decorating, celebrating, or keeping up with the traditions we once held dear. There's an unspoken expectation that holidays should be joyful, and when you can't summon that joy, it feels like a failure—

as if you're letting others down or even dishonoring the memory of the one you lost.

But over time, I've come to understand that it's okay to step back from traditions when grief feels overwhelming, redefine what the holidays mean, and say no to celebrations when they feel like too much. Grief doesn't take a holiday, and healing doesn't follow a calendar. It's a messy, complicated, and deeply personal journey.

Finding New Traditions

For some years, I haven't decorated at all. Other times, I've found ways to honor Bryant in a way that feels right:

- Lighting a candle in his memory.
- Hanging a unique ornament with his name on it.
- Creating a memory table with photos and keepsakes.
- Donating to a charity in his honor.
- Sharing stories about him around the table.

I've also found comfort in giving back. Instead of focusing on what's missing, I try to focus on helping others—supporting cancer charities or providing for families in need. These new traditions don't erase the pain but help me feel connected to Bryant meaningfully.

Words of Encouragement

To anyone grieving through birthdays, holidays, and milestones—you are not alone. It's okay to step back from celebrations that feel too painful. It's OK to skip decorating or change traditions. And celebrating in new ways is OK to honor your loved one. Grief doesn't come with rules, and healing doesn't follow a schedule.

God doesn't rush our grief or expect us to force smiles. He meets us where we are—whether surrounded by festive lights or sitting quietly in the dark.

As you navigate the holidays, hold tight to the memories. Speak their name. Light a candle. Cry when you need to. Laugh when you can. And trust that healing is not about forgetting but finding new ways to love and remember.

The Pain of Death Anniversaries—When the World Moves On

For many grieving parents, birthdays and holidays aren't the only hard days. Death anniversaries carry just as much weight—if not more. These days force us to relive the loss, the final moments, and the emptiness that followed.

It's painful to see the world move forward while your grief remains just as raw. Whether you spend the day surrounded by friends or reflecting alone, know that remembering is an act of love—and love never dies.

Bryant and his Uncle Jeff improvised when they could no longer go Black Friday shopping with things like this middle-of-the-night Whataburger run when Bryant was sick.

WHAT EVERY GRIEVING MOTHER WISHES YOU KNEW

Chapter 17
WHEN LIVING FEELS IMPOSSIBLE

Content Warning:

This chapter contains a personal account of suicidal thoughts and deep grief following the loss of a child. While it offers hope, healing, and spiritual encouragement, it may be difficult for some readers. Please take care while reading, and know that you are not alone.

If you or someone you know is struggling with suicidal thoughts, help is available. You can call or text the Suicide & Crisis Lifeline at 988—someone is there 24/7 to listen, support, and help you through.

"There were moments when dying felt easier than living without my son."

Grief has a way of leading you to dark places you never imagined. After Bryant died, I faced some of the darkest moments of my life. I wish I could say I always trusted God to carry me through, but the truth is, there were times when I didn't even want to keep going.

It's not easy to admit, especially as a Christian, but there were moments when dying felt easier than living without my son. The pain was so overwhelming that the thought of ending my life crossed my mind more times than I care to admit.

I never planned anything dramatic. I didn't think about guns or other violent means, but the idea of overdosing on pills seemed like a quiet way to make the pain stop. I spent months barely functioning. I couldn't get out of bed. My feet never felt so heavy or hurt so much. The only thing I could do was cry. Deep, endless, loud sobs kept me tethered to my wet pillow. During that time, the thought of slipping away in my sleep felt more comforting than waking up to face another day without Bryant. The emotional, spiritual, and physical pain was unbearable, and it felt impossible to survive, let alone pull myself out of even to try to better myself.

The Breaking Point

About three years after Bryant died, I worked with FEMA (Federal Emergency Management Agency), traveling to different states for extended periods to access homes and businesses after natural disasters. It was my first time back to work, which was rewarding helping others, but it also separated me from Austin for months, leaving me feeling more alone than ever. Everyone thought I was doing great. I did as well. I was flying here and there, appearing as if I was thriving. But I wasn't. I was silently dying.

One day, I reached a breaking point. I was utterly exhausted—physically, emotionally, and spiritually. While on assignment in Panama City, I drove to the beach to clear my head. Bryant and I had always loved the beach. It was our happy place, and standing there at the water's edge, I could almost feel him with me.

But as I stood there, staring at the waves, I felt a pull that scared me. I had the strongest urge to walk into the water until it covered me completely. I knew I wasn't a strong enough swimmer to fight the current, and at that moment, I wasn't sure I even wanted to.

The weight of losing Bryant, my parents, and the distance from Austin hit me all at once. It felt like more than I could bear, and I didn't want to keep fighting. I was done.

God's Intervention

As I inched closer to the water's edge, God intervened with the words of Jeremiah 29:11- *"For I know the plans I have for you,"* declares the Lord. *"plans to prosper you and not to harm you, plans to give hope and a future."* God gave me this verse just before we moved to Georgia, away from family and friends, and a good while before Bryant's birth, amid all the betrayal I was facing. For those two years in Georgia, that verse was an everyday part of my life, whether in a card in the mail, a sermon, a message from a friend, or a book I was reading. God knew what I needed before I even knew there was a problem. When Bryant was diagnosed, I realized just how vital that verse was and how God began preparing me before he was born. In all his infinite wisdom and mercy, he knew what I would need. God reminded me of Bryant's courage in his fight to live and that I needed to fight for my life. And, finally, God reminded me of Austin, what a great blessing he was, and how much I loved him. That made me think about Austin's pain after losing Bryant and how he needed me, even if he didn't always show it.

God also reminded me of my faith. I knew, deep down, that taking my life wouldn't erase the pain—it would only pass it on to the people I loved most. The thought of leaving Austin with that kind of grief was enough to pull me back.

I stepped away from the water and back toward life. That moment didn't erase my pain, but it gave me clarity. God wasn't finished with me yet. I had more to live for—even if I couldn't see it then. I knew God could, and that was enough to give me light in the darkness.

As you will read in Chapter 26, I was in a similar situation while working with FEMA in Miami before this incident. It wasn't planned or even a thought, but the result of medication intended to help me through my emotions. Thankfully, God had gone ahead of me and made a way to survive.

A Spiritual Battle

"Grief can make death look like the only escape, but that's a lie from the enemy."

Looking back, I know Satan was working overtime in my grief. The Bible warns us in John 10:10 that *"The thief comes only to steal, kill and destroy."* That's exactly what Satan tried to do—steal my hope, kill my faith, and destroy my life.

But God is stronger and more powerful than any lie Satan can whisper. II Corinthians 10:5 reminds us to *"take captive every thought to make it obedient to Christ."* That's what I had to do. I had to drown out the enemy's lies with the truth of God's Word, even when it felt impossible to believe.

A Message for Others Struggling

If you've ever felt the pain that makes you want to give up, I want you to know I see you. Grief can make death look like the only escape, but that's a lie from the enemy. God created you with a purpose; your story isn't over yet. I know it's hard. I see how the weight of loss feels unbearable. But there is hope—even when you can't see it. If you're struggling with suicidal thoughts, please don't keep it to yourself. Contact someone you trust—a friend, pastor, counselor, or even a hotline. You don't have to fight this battle alone.

And if you've lost someone to suicide, I want you to know that it's not your fault. The enemy wants you to carry the blame, but God offers grace. Let Him take the weight of your pain.

A Final Word of Encouragement

Grief is a battle, but you don't have to fight it alone. God is with you and has surrounded you with people who want to help.

If you're reading this and feel like you're drowning, take my story as proof that you can come back up for air. Life can feel impossible after loss, but it's still worth living.

Hold on. Reach out. And trust that God will meet you right where you are— even if it's at the water's edge.

I would have missed all these wonderful moments—such beauty from ashes.

Chapter 18
IMPACT OF GRIEF ON MARRIAGE

When a child dies, the pain is immeasurable. Yet, the experience of grief can differ dramatically depending on whether one faces that loss alone or with a partner by one's side. I never experienced that firsthand, as I was divorced, and I know the sting of being alone all too well.

Research indicates that the death of a child can either strain or strengthen a marriage, depending on various factors. Some couples find solace in shared grief, while others may struggle due to differing grieving styles.

The Power of Partnership

In a marriage, the loss of a child creates a dual burden as each partner carries their pain while also relying on one another for comfort. Research from grief support organizations like *GriefShare* tells us that married couples often find that their shared grief can either bring them closer together or, if unaddressed, widen the emotional gap between them when partners grieve in harmony. They can lean on one another for strength, communicate their needs, and even find moments of solace in the shared remembrance of their child. The presence of a spouse—someone to hold onto, cry with, or sit in silence with—can be a lifeline.

Even the simplest acts of intimacy, like a shared meal, a quiet conversation before bed, or a hug, can remind them that they are not facing their darkest hours alone.

A spouse's physical closeness and emotional support help create a buffer against the overwhelming isolation that often accompanies such a loss—a very stark contrast to someone like me.

Shared Burdens, Different Journeys

I recall many times when my brother, who also lost a child, would insist that I wasn't alone in my grief. His words, meant to comfort me, sometimes struck a nerve. He had the benefit of a partner—his wife—who would listen, hold him, and provide that essential human warmth when the pain became too much to bear.

In contrast, I often found myself facing my grief alone. I would lie awake in a quiet room, the only sound of which was the faint hum of the television, wishing desperately for a comforting presence. The absence of a partner to share in my sorrow deepened my loneliness. I longed for someone to hold my hand—or hold me.

At times, I felt anger at being alone, but I later realized that each person's grief journey is as unique as their relationship with the one they lost. Even for married couples, grief can look different for each partner. One might openly express their emotions, while the other internalizes their pain. These differences, if unacknowledged, can lead to frustration and misunderstanding. However, they can also become opportunities for deeper connection and healing when approached with patience and compassion.

A friend and fellow author I met years ago before Bryant's diagnosis read an advanced copy of this book before publication. I value **Amelia Frahm's** insight and opinions as she has a college degree in journalism, has published two books of her own, and provided valuable input throughout, for which I am grateful.

She brought something to my attention regarding this chapter I didn't think of. Even though married, some men and women may feel just as alone as I did being single because they were not getting the support they needed from their spouses sharing the same living space with them. Sometimes, that loneliness can be just as intense as being single is. Thinking back, I experienced it in my marriage through my pregnancy with Bryant and the five-plus years I chose to stay following his birth.

Learning from Support Resources

GriefShare and similar support programs emphasize that mourning is a deeply personal process—multifaceted and without a one-size-fits-all solution. For couples, a crucial part of healing is learning to communicate about their loss without judgment. Some find that openly discussing their feelings strengthens their bond, while others benefit from seeking counseling together to navigate the complex emotions that come with losing a child.

One standard piece of advice from *GriefShare* is the importance of creating a safe space for grieving—where both partners feel free to express their pain without fear of burdening the other. This safe space might take different forms: a weekly check-in, a prayer session, or even participation in a structured support group for grieving parents. What matters most is that both partners recognize their individual experiences of loss as valid and understand that supporting one another—through honest, sometimes raw communication—is a vital part of healing.

A Personal Reflection on Isolation

Though I never experienced the comfort of a spouse's presence during my darkest times, I watched my brother and his wife navigate their shared grief. I often resented my brother's advice after Bryant died because he had a partner to lean on when they lost their daughter —it was the kind of solace I longed for but was never afforded. That isolation remains one of the most painful aspects of grief for me—the stark contrast between having someone to hold you and facing sorrow alone.

Common Challenges Couples Face After Loss

Differing Grieving Processes: No two people grieve the same way. One partner may seek external support while the other turns inward, creating a sense of emotional distance.

Communication Barriers: Grief can make open dialogue difficult, leading to misunderstandings or feelings of neglect.

Emotional Withdrawal: Overwhelming pain may cause one or both partners to retreat inward, making it difficult to offer or receive support.

Embracing Healing Together

For couples experiencing the devastating loss of a child, the road ahead is difficult—but it can also be an opportunity to rebuild and strengthen your bond. Here are a few ways to navigate this painful journey together:

Strategies for Navigating Grief as a Couple

Lean on Faith: For many couples, faith becomes a cornerstone of the healing process.

Allow your shared beliefs to guide you—pray together, seek comfort in scripture, and trust that God's plan will lead you forward, even in sorrow.

Communicate Openly: Grief looks different for everyone. Acknowledge that you and your partner may grieve differently, and make space for honest conversations—even if that means sitting together in silence. Sometimes, knowing your partner is present, even in their pain, can be deeply comforting.

Seek Professional Support: Consider marriage counseling or joining a support group for couples who have lost a child. A trained counselor can provide guidance and strategies to help you navigate the overwhelming emotions that arise after loss.

Join a Support Group: Organizations like *GriefShare* offer sessions where couples can connect with others who genuinely understand their pain. I've attended individual counseling with Christian counselors, but nothing helped me as much as the *GriefShare* meetings. Based on my personal experience, it remains my number-one recommendation.

Establish New Traditions: Consider creating new traditions that honor your child's memory. This could include a special meal on their birthday or a quiet evening of reflection on significant anniversaries. These rituals can help keep your child's memory alive while strengthening the bond between you and your partner.

A Call to Couples in Grief

To the married couples who have lost a child, know that while your grief may sometimes feel like a burden too heavy to bear, you have a partner to share that load. Even when you grieve differently, your love for each other and your child can be the bridge that brings healing. Remember that healing is not a race but a journey taken one day at a time, side by side.

I hope this chapter can serve as a reminder that, even amid the most overwhelming sorrow, there is strength to be found in unity. You are not alone in your pain, and together, you can honor your child's memory while finding the support and love you both need.

Encouragement for Couples

To those walking this horrific path together: lean into each other. Recognize that grief may manifest differently for each of you, and that's okay. Offer patience, understanding, and grace. Seek external support when needed, and remember, it's possible to find a new rhythm together, even after such a profound loss.

Lost Siblings

Austin & Bryant

Meredith & Reagan

Reagan and Meredith with Granny Little, my mom

Anna & Travis

Lost Siblings

Kierra and Kody with Kena

Kody and Kierra with Kena

Delaney & Johann

Chapter 19
SIBLINGS: THE SILENT SURVIVORS

"... his words reveal the anxiety he carries—the unspoken fears that Bryant's story might somehow repeat itself in his own life."

Grief is often most visible in parents who lose a child, but the silent burden of loss also weighs heavily on the siblings left behind. Whether they are young children, teenagers, or adults, siblings experience grief in deeply personal ways that often go unspoken.

For my son, Austin, losing his younger brother, Bryant, wasn't just about losing a sibling—it was the loss of a lifelong bond, shared memories, and dreams of the future. But like many siblings, Austin grieved quietly, keeping his pain private while navigating adulthood.

Austin's Quiet Grief

Austin was 25 years old when Bryant died—an age when he was balancing work, college, and the responsibilities of adulthood. While Bryant and I were in and out of the hospital, Austin's life looked very different. He wasn't immersed in the daily battles in the same way I was, but he visited as often as he could, carefully balancing his own life with the harsh reality of Bryant's illness.

Even after Bryant's death, Austin remained guarded. He didn't cry openly or talk much about his feelings. Instead, he carried his grief internally, processing it in ways that weren't always visible. Years later, after getting married and starting a family, he finally began to open up to his wife about the profound impact Bryant's death had on him.

I've often wondered if his privacy was a defense mechanism—a way to shield himself from the overwhelming emotions that grief brings. He assured me it wasn't. At times, his reserved approach has made me feel disconnected from his journey, but I've come to respect that Austin's grief is his own.

Unspoken Fears

"I allow myself to feel that grief because it is a reminder of the love I have for her."

What's most challenging for me is knowing that Bryant's cancer and death still weigh heavily on Austin's mind. When Bryant was first diagnosed, doctors suggested genetic testing to determine if Austin was also at risk. But in the chaos of battling Bryant's cancer, we never pursued it.

Now, as an adult, the decision is Austin's to make, and I know the fear of cancer still lingers within him. He has made passing comments about his health and weight, often saying, "I'm not trying to get cancer or have a heart attack." Those words cut deeply because they expose the anxiety he carries—the unspoken fear that Bryant's story might somehow repeat itself in his own life.

Recently, Austin confided that he had come to terms with Bryant's fate during his cancer fight. Like all of us, he hoped for a miracle but admitted he had known Bryant would not survive.

"Some people wouldn't understand this, but after he passed and in the years that followed, I felt relief," Austin said. "Sadness, yes, but relief as well. Relief that he wasn't in pain anymore and that he could be normal again in heaven." He continued, "Relief that my living family could try to regain some resemblance of normalcy."

He explained that his goal as the healthy sibling was to ensure no one worried about him. He wanted me to focus entirely on Bryant and his needs.

Grief at Every Age

Austin's grief was different because he was an adult when his brother died, but younger siblings process loss in ways that can be just as complex.

My niece, Meredith, experienced the loss of her sister much earlier in life—at just nine years old.

"I was old enough to understand what death meant fully," Meredith said. "But at nine, I didn't grasp what would happen to her belongings. When my parents told me they were taking Reagan off life support, my immediate thought was about her things—her pink leather beanbag, her clothes, her Beanie Babies (which she never let me touch), her books. What would happen to them? It's a reflection of how young I was, navigating such a monumental, earth-shattering loss. At that age, those were the things that mattered most."

The reality of her sister's death didn't take long to sink in, though. Meredith first felt its weight on the drive home from the hospital the night Reagan passed.

"A complete person was missing," Meredith said. "This was the new normal. There was an empty seat wherever we went. An empty bedroom. A void that was so loud and visceral for my parents and me, yet invisible to others."

For Meredith, the way people reacted after Reagan's death was one of the hardest parts. She described it as almost embarrassing.

"I didn't want sympathy; I just wanted things to feel normal," she said.

But it wasn't just other people's reactions that affected her—seeing her parents grieve was just as difficult.

"As an only child now, I wasn't equipped emotionally to handle such a tragedy," Meredith said. "I just wanted everyone to be okay. I had never seen my parents cry like that before Reagan's passing—full-on, doubled-over weeping. It's indescribable to watch your heroes—your parents, who seem unbreakable and immortal—completely fall apart."

Today, as an adult, Meredith says grief looks different to her.

"It's an ache that comes during milestones—my wedding, Reagan's 30th birthday, seeing her friends announce engagements or pregnancies," she said. "But I allow myself to feel that grief because it's a reminder of the love I have for her."

Delaney was 11 years old when her older brother, Johann, passed away just two days before Bryant, also due to cancer. She had always seen him as her protector, and losing him left a void no one else could fill.

Though wise beyond her years, Delaney still needed space to feel like a kid. After our children died, I spent weekends away with Delaney and her mom, Connie, in Destin. Those trips allowed Delaney to laugh, share stories, and feel connected—without the pressure to "be strong." Her openness and ability to express her emotions have inspired me and everyone around her.

One of her greatest challenges was returning to school and being expected to act as if nothing had happened. Delaney said she lost friends because she could no longer relate to them. Their conversations revolved around things she now saw as trivial compared to the devastating loss of her brother.

Then there's **Kierra Spivey**, who was 14 when she lost her baby sister, Kena. I met her family in the hospital 10 years ago, and our friendship became more like family. Watching Kierra grow up without Kena has been bittersweet.

Though she doesn't always speak openly about her grief, Kierra carries a depth of compassion and strength that can only come from walking through tragedy. In the early years after losing Kena, she struggled with extreme anxiety, spending most of her days crying and unable to get out of bed. Eventually, she sought counseling, which helped her tremendously. She's doing much better today—working three jobs and in a relationship. It has been so good to see her finding her way after a loss that reshaped her family's world in every way imaginable.

The Struggles Siblings Face

Siblings often feel like the forgotten mourners. With so much attention focused on parents, their grief may unintentionally go unnoticed. They might experience:

- **Guilt** for surviving when their sibling didn't.
- **Loneliness** from losing a sibling and part of their identity.
- **Pressure** to stay strong for their grieving parents.
- **Fear** of the future—especially when the death was due to illness or genetics.
- **Anger** at God, family, or the world for not preventing the loss.

Children and teens may also struggle with emotions they can't fully articulate. They might act out, withdraw, or experience anxiety about losing others they love. Meanwhile, adult siblings often bury their grief, trying not to add to their parents' pain.

A Word of Encouragement

To parents: Don't overlook the siblings. Their grief may look different, but it's no less valid. Encourage open conversations, but don't force them. Sometimes, just acknowledging their loss is enough.

To siblings: Your grief matters. You don't have to carry it alone or hide it to protect others. Please find comfort in friends, family, or a counselor. Know that it's okay to lean on others.

To everyone: Grief is not a one-size-fits-all journey. It's messy, personal, and unique for each person. But with time, faith, and connection, healing is possible.

Honoring the Bonds That Remain

Siblings often share an irreplaceable bond built on shared memories, secrets, and dreams. When that bond is broken by death, it leaves an emptiness that's hard to fill. However, siblings can keep that bond alive by honoring their loved one's memory by sharing stories, celebrating birthdays, and speaking their name.

To every sibling grieving in silence: Your story matters. Your grief matters. And your love will always be enough.

Chapter 20
A BOND FORGED IN GRIEF

Grief is an isolating journey, but God often provides us with unexpected connections—lifelines that help carry us through. Those connections came through two extraordinary women—**Dawn D. Spivey** and **Connie Lee**—whose friendships have been instrumental in my journey toward hope and healing.

We often hear that grief is something we must face alone, but I've learned the opposite is true. God places people in our lives to walk alongside us, reminding us that we are not alone. These relationships don't erase the pain, but they soften it. They bring light to the darkest days and reveal God's faithfulness, even in the valley.

A Bond Born in the Hospital

Dawn's daughter, **Kena**, was just 11 months old when Bryant and I met them in the hospital. Born with cancer, Kena faced an uphill battle from the start. Yet, she was a radiant light, her smile breaking through the shadows of sickness. We quickly called her our **"sunshine in the storm."**

Kena and Bryant formed an immediate and unexplainable bond that transcended their vast age difference. Though Bryant was 17 and Kena was barely a toddler, they became kindred spirits, bound by shared hospital stays and chemotherapy schedules. Watching them together was like witnessing hope in motion. They lifted each other in ways that words could never capture, and in doing so, they lifted the rest of us—reminding us that even in the most brutal battles, God's love was still at work.

Their bond laid the foundation for a lifelong friendship between Dawn and me. We were two mothers navigating the terrifying world of childhood cancer, leaning on each other when we were too weak to stand alone. Dawn's love, support, and understanding carried me through moments I could not have faced alone.

Dawn's husband, **Charles**, was just as supportive and became a great friend to Bryant. When we weren't in the hospital, they continually texted, or we were all together. I'm thankful Charles was there for Bryant. Their friendship meant a lot to us both.

Our connection didn't end when our children's battles did. It continues today as we carry their memories forward, honoring their lives and sharing our stories to offer hope to others. Kena passed away on September 28, 2016, two months before my son, at just two years old.

Two Losses, One Day Apart

Then there's Connie—another woman whose story intertwined with mine in a way only God could orchestrate. Connie's son, Johann, was 16 when he lost his battle with cancer on the morning before Thanksgiving 2016—just one day before Bryant took his last breath.

Like me, Connie was navigating unimaginable grief as a single mother, trying to hold herself together while her world fell apart. Our experiences mirrored each other so closely that we formed an instant connection—one grounded in loss, faith, and the shared hope of Heaven. Connie and I became each other's anchors on the most challenging days. When the weight of grief felt unbearable, we reminded one another that our sons were whole and healed in Heaven.

Finding Hope in Shared Healing

The relationships I've formed with Dawn and Connie have shown me that healing doesn't mean forgetting—it means finding ways to honor the lives of those we've lost. Through their friendship, I've been reminded that even amid devastating grief, there can be moments of peace, joy, and connection.

Our weekends together have become sacred. They aren't just about escaping the day-to-day reality of grief; they're about rebuilding pieces of ourselves and celebrating the lives of the children we lost.

I'll never forget our shared moments—laughing at memories and crying over milestones our children will never reach. In these sacred spaces of remembrance, I have felt God's presence the most—through the love and understanding of women who truly know the depths of my pain.

Hope Rooted in God's Promises

One verse that has given me comfort is Isaiah 43:2: *"When you pass through the waters, I will be with you, and when you pass through the rivers, they will not sweep over you. When you walk through the fire, you will not be burned; the flames will not set you ablaze."*

This verse reminds me that God doesn't promise to spare us from the waters or the fire—but He does promise to walk us through them. I've seen that truth reflected in the friendships He has placed in my life.

A Word of Encouragement

To anyone walking this road of grief, I want you to know that peace is possible. It doesn't come all at once, and it doesn't erase the pain. But through faith, connection, and time, healing takes root.

Lean into God's promises. Let Him carry you when you can't carry yourself. Surround yourself with people who understand your pain and will walk with you through it.

Ecclesiastes 4:9-10 says:

"Two are better than one because they have a good return for their labor: If either of them falls down, one can help the other up."

We aren't meant to walk through grief alone. God provides people—friends, family, and even strangers—who become His hands and feet in our lives. **Let them in.**

Better Together

Dawn and Janet

Janet and Theresa

Delaney and Janet

Connie and Janet

Kierra and Janet

Chapter 21
MUSIC IN THE NIGHT

"The same God I sang about as a child—the God of mercy and miracles was still with me, even in my sorrow."

Grief has a way of creeping in during the night. The world grows quiet, but your mind does not. It races with memories, questions, regrets, and fears.

After Bryant died, nights became the hardest hours of my life. I couldn't sleep. I couldn't focus. And I certainly couldn't pray the way I wanted to. All I did was cry.

I often sat awake in the dark, consumed by the weight of my loss, searching for anything that might bring me comfort. That's when I stumbled upon a Facebook post that would change everything.

A Song That Changed Everything

A friend, **Lisa Martinez Moretz**, had started sharing videos of her daughter, **Melissa**, playing old hymns late at night on the piano. Lisa explained that when she couldn't sleep, she found peace listening to her daughter pour her heart out to God through music.

I don't remember the first song I heard Melissa play, but I remember breaking down in tears as the opening notes filled the room. It felt like a balm to my soul—something familiar in the unfamiliar landscape of my grief.

At first, I sang along quietly. Then, as the words came back to me, I sang louder. Suddenly, the music wasn't just a song but a prayer.

The old hymns carried me back to my childhood and the pews of the churches where my dad preached. They were woven into the fabric of my upbringing—steady and unchanging, even when my world had fallen apart.

Melissa's music broke through my grief. God used Melissa and Lisa, their talent, and a piano to remind me of His presence and grace. The same God I sang about as a child—the God of mercy and miracles—was still with me, even in my sorrow.

When Worship Becomes Prayer

The more I listened, the more I felt connected to God again. Those hymns filled the space where my prayers had failed. They reminded me of Psalm 42:8—*"By day the Lord directs His love, at night His song is with me—a prayer to the God of my life."*

Eventually, I sent Lisa a private message to thank her for sharing this precious gift. I told her she had no idea what a blessing she had been to me and probably many others. Her response left me speechless.

She told me that Bryant's life and faith had inspired her.

Her words warmed my heart. I had prayed for God to use Bryant's life, even in his death, and here was evidence that those prayers were being answered. Bryant's faith had reached far beyond what I could have imagined, and now, this woman's music was returning to comfort me. God used her obedience in sharing the music to fill a void I didn't know how to express. I couldn't pray, but I could sing. I couldn't speak, but I could listen. And through it all, God met me there.

When Roles Reverse—Comfort in Her Grief

Unfortunately, grief doesn't stay confined to one person. Two years after Bryant died, Lisa and her husband, **James**, faced their tragedy when their 31-year-old daughter, **Lydia Brianne Moretz**, was killed in a car accident on March 3, 2018, in Pensacola, FL.

Lydia left behind twin girls in elementary school, and suddenly, this lady— who had comforted me through her music—was now raising her granddaughters while walking through her devastating grief. I was heartbroken for her. I knew the depths of her pain and marveled at how God had unknowingly prepared her for this moment through the music she shared with others.

Seeing God's hand in both of our stories was humbling—how He used Bryant's life to touch Lisa's faith and how He used Lisa's faith to comfort me. Now, He was equipping her to carry her granddaughters through their grief, just as He had taken me.

I had witnessed how God's grace moved in cycles of comfort. Bryant's faith inspired her to return to worship. Her music ministered to me in my grief. And now, she was able to offer support to her granddaughters as she faced her unimaginable loss.

I considered how God prepares us for moments we can't see coming. When she decided to share the songs she was ministering to me, Lisa didn't know that one day, she would face a loss that mirrored my own. And I didn't know, when I reached out to thank her, that she would someday need comfort through the very same grief that once consumed me. But God knew.

Worship as a Lifeline

This experience opened my eyes to the unexpected ways God sustains us during grief. Sometimes, He speaks through scripture. Sometimes, He responds in prayer. And sometimes, He uses a piano and an old hymn in the middle of the night.

Music reaches places in our hearts that words cannot. It becomes a prayer when words fail and a reminder of God's presence when we feel alone. In those moments, I learned that worship isn't just about praising God in the good times—it's about clinging to Him when life feels unbearable. Like the melody I heard in the stillness of the night, grief has its own rhythm—a rise and fall that can feel unpredictable and overwhelming. But through it all, God's song remains.

A Word to the Weary

I've come to believe that worship is one of the purest forms of prayer. It doesn't require eloquence—only surrender. God hears us whether we raise our voices in praise or whisper through tears. And sometimes, He answers by sending someone like Lisa to remind us that even in the darkest night, His song is still playing.

Let music become your prayer if you're in the depths of grief and struggling to pray. Let the lyrics of hymns and worship songs fill the silence. Don't be afraid to cry through the words or sing through the tears. Grief may try to silence you, but worship will remind you that God hasn't left. He is still near.

Let Psalm 40:3 encourage you: *"He put a new song in my mouth, a hymn of praise to our God. Many will see and fear the Lord and put their trust in Him."*

God will give you a new song, even in your sorrow. And in time, that song will become a lifeline—not just for you, but for others who need to know they aren't alone. Keep singing. Keep trusting, even in the darkest night.

PART 4

LIVING WITH LOSS

Chapter 22
MY DAD'S SERMONS

"In so many of his sermons, it was as if he was speaking directly to me like we were in the same room."

I was struck by how many of my dad's sermons focused on themes that have shaped my journey—grief, guilt, forgiveness, faith, prayer, and hope. Though he wrote them decades ago, reading them now feels like he's speaking directly to me.

When my niece passed away in 2001, my brother could call Mom and Dad anytime for comfort, advice, or wisdom. I didn't have that opportunity, as they had both passed before Bryant. Through my dad's sermons, I found his guidance and reassurance in my grief. He spoke directly to me in many of his messages as if we were sitting together in the same room. I even discovered one sermon about terminal illness—it was as if he had known all along.

I've never been more grateful to have been raised by godly parents who shaped my faith. Dad was a man of unwavering faith. He and my mom prayed daily for me and my brothers, asking for God's favor over our lives. Now, as I navigate the depths of loss, I believe their prayers continue to cover me—even in my grief.

As I prepared to write this book, one sermon stood out. It was titled **"Why Me, Lord?"** In it, my dad shared ten biblical reasons why Christians suffer. As I read his words, it felt as if God Himself was answering the questions that had consumed me since Bryant's passing.

I want to share those lessons here because they've brought comfort, perspective, and a deeper understanding of God's purpose—even in suffering.

1. We Suffer Because of Sin

"Sin is disobedience to God," my dad wrote. *"And suffering can be redemptive—it is God's love in action, calling us to turn back to Him."*

Key Scriptures:

"Sanctify yourselves therefore, and be ye holy: for I am the Lord your God." — Leviticus 20:7 (KJV)

"For the wages of sin is death, but the gift of God is eternal life through Jesus Christ our Lord." — Romans 6:23 (KJV)

While I never blamed Bryant's illness on sin, I wrestled with guilt after his passing—wondering if I had failed him or if my prayers had fallen short. But my dad's words reminded me that suffering isn't always about punishment. Sometimes, it refines us, draws us closer to God, and deepens our dependence on Him.

2. We Suffer Because of Obedience to God

This point surprised me. How could obedience lead to suffering? Shouldn't following God protect us from pain?

Key Scripture:

"Everyone who wants to live godly in Christ Jesus will be persecuted." — 2 Timothy 3:12 (NIV)

Dad explained that obedience often puts us at odds with the world, leading to challenges, persecution, and trials. Bryant's faith never wavered, even as his illness worsened. He trusted God's plan and continued to show love and kindness. His suffering wasn't meaningless—it pointed others to Christ, just as my dad's sermon said it could.

3. We Suffer Because of Foolish Choices

Dad taught us that some suffering stems from our own mistakes. He referenced Samson's story in Judges 16, illustrating how unwise choices led to betrayal and captivity.

Key Scripture:

"For the wages of sin is death, but the gift of God is eternal life through Christ Jesus our Lord." — Romans 6:23 (KJV)

Though choices didn't cause Bryant's illness, I struggled with self-blame after his passing. My dad's sermon reminded me that God's grace is greater than our failures—and He never abandons us, even when we fall short.

4. We Suffer to Shift Our Focus to Heaven

Suffering forces us to loosen our grip on the temporary and fix our eyes on what is eternal.

Key Scripture:

"Set your minds on things above, not on earthly things." — Colossians 3:2 (NIV)

Bryant's faith gave him peace about heaven. He spoke of it as if it were just around the corner—close and welcoming. His confidence also challenged me to shift my focus.

5. We Suffer to Prepare for a Greater Purpose

Dad used Joseph's story (Genesis 39–41) to illustrate how God uses suffering to prepare us for something greater. Joseph endured betrayal, slavery, and imprisonment before God elevated him to save nations during a famine.

Like Joseph, I don't know how God will use my grief. But writing this book—and sharing Bryant's story—already feels like part of that purpose.

6. We Suffer to Glorify God

Key Scripture:

"This sickness will not end in death… it is for God's glory so that God's Son may be glorified through it." — John 11:4 (NIV)

My dad's words reminded me that Bryant's faith glorified God. Even in his suffering, Bryant's testimony pointed others to Jesus—showing God's presence in every step of his journey.

7. We Suffer to Develop Compassion

Jesus' suffering gave Him the ability to empathize with our weaknesses.

Key Scripture:

"For we do not have a high priest who is unable to empathize with our weaknesses, but we have one who has been tempted in every way—just as we are." — Hebrews 4:15 (NIV)

Grief has made me more tender toward those who are hurting. My dad's sermon reminded me that compassion grows from shared suffering and that God uses it to comfort others.

8. We Suffer as a Test of Faith

The story of Job shows that suffering reveals the sincerity of our faith.

Key Scripture:

"The Lord gave and the Lord has taken away; blessed be the name of the Lord." — Job 1:21 (NIV)

Bryant's faith, like Job's, never wavered. Even in pain, he trusted God, proving that faith isn't about what God gives—it's about who He is.

9. We Suffer to Remain Humble

Paul's "thorn in the flesh" reminded him to rely on God's grace rather than his strength.

Key Scripture:

"My grace is sufficient for you, for my power is made perfect in weakness." — 2 Corinthians 12:9 (NIV)

Bryant's strength came from his abilities and God's grace. Watching his faith in weakness reminded me to lean on God as well.

10. We Suffer to Refine Our Faith

Suffering is like refining gold—it burns away impurities and strengthens what remains.

Key Scripture:

"Do not be surprised at the fiery ordeal that has come on you to test you... But rejoice... that you may be overjoyed when His glory is revealed." — 1 Peter 4:12-13 (NIV)

My dad's words challenged me to let grief refine me, not destroy me. He once said, *"Trials can make us bitter or better."* I choose to let God make me better.

Suffering is like refining gold— it burns away impurities and strengthens what remains."

A Final Reflection

Reflecting on my dad's sermon and Bryant's life, I see how suffering shaped their faith. Neither of them saw their pain as meaningless. Instead, they trusted God to use it for His glory.

Their faith inspires me to keep going, even when grief feels heavy. As I continue this journey, I pray their stories—and this book—remind others that hope and healing are possible, even in the darkest moments.

To Those Who Grieve

If you're reading this and your heart aches with the pain of loss—whether it's a child, parent, sibling, or friend—I want you to know you're not alone. I know what it feels like to have your world shattered, to wake up wondering how you'll keep breathing, and to fall asleep with tears soaking your pillow.

I know the fear of forgetting their voice, the guilt over unspoken words, and the ache of wanting just one more hug, one more laugh, one more moment. I know what it's like to question God, to feel anger, and to wrestle with guilt, regret, and despair.

But I also know this—God is near. He doesn't turn away from your tears or your questions. He isn't intimidated by your anger or brokenness. He meets you right where you are—even in the darkest valleys. He holds you when you can't stand and whispers the truth when you're drowning in lies. You are not forgotten. Your child is not forgotten. Your love for them and God's love for you will never end. Even in the depths of grief, there is hope.

Healing Doesn't Mean Forgetting

Grief has no timeline, and healing doesn't mean letting go. It's okay to cry, smile, talk about them, and keep their memory alive in whatever way brings you comfort.

Sharing Bryant's story has helped me heal, and I encourage you to find ways to honor your loved one. Whether through journaling, scrapbooks, speaking their name, or serving others in their memory—your love can continue to make an impact.

"Celebrating Reagan's life has been a source of healing for me," my niece Meredith shared about her sister. *"Whether through tattoos, framed photos, social media posts, or dressing fabulously on her birthday, these acts bring me joy. To anyone grieving, I encourage you to find ways to celebrate your loved ones. Paint, sing, or write about them. Even as I write this, I think about how proud Reagan would be of me. Celebrating her is healing in ways I never imagined."*

Grief doesn't disappear—it becomes something we carry differently over time. It softens, making space for joy again—not because we've forgotten, but because love is resilient.

You're Allowed to Grieve in Your Way

Don't let anyone tell you how to grieve. There is no "right way" to endure this pain. Grieve publicly or privately. Speak their name often or hold it close to your heart. Cry every day or not at all. Your grief is as unique as your love, and it is valid—no matter how it appears to others.

Surround yourself with people who understand. Find those who will sit with you in silence, cry with you without trying to fix it, and say your child's name without hesitation. And if you can't find those people right now, know that God is already with you. He will never leave.

A Promise of Reunion

I don't know what brought you to this book—whether you're a grieving parent like me, a friend trying to support someone through loss, or simply searching for hope. But I want you to remember this: This is not the end of the story.

Revelation 21:4 promises, *"He will wipe every tear from their eyes. There will be no more death or mourning or crying or pain."*

A day is coming when every tear will be wiped away, every heartache will be healed, and we will be reunited with those we've lost. Until then, we walk by faith, holding onto the promise that God is preparing a place where grief and loss will no longer exist.

Keep Moving Forward

To every grieving mother reading this—I see you. I feel your pain. And I believe in your strength, even if you don't feel strong right now. Take it one breath at a time. Lean into God's grace. Allow yourself to grieve, to feel, and to heal.

You don't have to have it all figured out. You have to keep moving forward— one shaky step at a time.

You are not alone. You are loved. You are seen. And even in grief, there is hope.

My parent's, Thomas and Joyce Carnley Little

WHAT EVERY GRIEVING MOTHER WISHES YOU KNEW

Chapter 23
PEACE IN COMPLETE HEALING

"...as much as it hurts not to have him here,
I find peace in knowing he is free..."

Even though I knew Bryant was dying and that his healing wouldn't happen this side of Heaven, I was still in disbelief and shock when the time came for him to leave. I found myself waiting to hear his truck pull into the driveway and his cheerful voice announcing his arrival at the front door—even though I knew it wasn't possible. All I could think about was how badly Bryant wanted to live and how desperately I wanted that for him, too.

Wrestling with God's Plan

Looking back, I am in awe of how Bryant planned every detail of his final days, a process I wrote about earlier in this book. But even though I knew it was exactly what he wanted, I still wrestled with it deeply in the days following his passing.

Because of his age and maturity, Bryant made all his medical decisions. He knew where he wanted to be, who he wanted by his side, and how he wanted his final days to unfold. The hospital staff honored his every request.

And while it was a profound act of love that he gave me, it didn't make it any easier to accept once he was gone.

The Hard Path to Peace

There were moments when I wondered if I would ever find peace after such a devastating loss. But over time, I've seen the completeness of God's healing in Bryant's story.

Part of this peace came as I continued to follow the families we met in the hospital—families fighting the same battle, though with different types of cancer. Some of their children survived, but their lives are far from "normal." Parents of survivors have shared the constant monitoring, the anxiety of every doctor's visit, and the lifelong fear that cancer could return. It's a weight they carry daily. In the childhood cancer world, we call this the "new normal."

I can't imagine the toll that must take on a family or a child who has already endured so much. I don't know if I would have survived that kind of endless uncertainty—waiting for the following scan, holding my breath for the next test.

I know the parents of survivors are beyond grateful for their child's life, and I am for them as well. But the next doctor's appointment—and what it will reveal—is always in their minds. Many describe it as never being able to exhale or feel safe fully.

Bryant was spared from that, and as much as it hurts not to have him here, I find peace in knowing he is free—free from suffering, fear, and the weight of what might have been. That realization doesn't erase my grief but helps soften its sharp edges.

Trusting God's Plan

Over the years, I've come to trust that God's plan for Bryant wasn't just for the time he spent here with us—it extends to the eternity he is now experiencing in Heaven. His healing wasn't what I prayed for, but it was what God knew was best for him.

That trust didn't come quickly, but it has brought me peace. It's a *peace that passeth all understanding* (Philippians 4:7)—the peace that reassures me that Bryant is whole, restored, and free—knowing that truth has become my anchor, hope, and strength.

I think back to the nights in the hospital when Bryant and I would pray for strength, knowing we were running out of time but still holding onto hope. Those prayers weren't in vain. They gave us the courage to face what was ahead and the comfort of knowing God was with us every step of the way.

Encouragement for Other Parents

To the parents reading this who are walking through the unimaginable pain of losing a child, I want to offer you this hope: peace can come. It may take time, and it may not look the way you expect, but it is possible to find solace in the completeness of your child's healing.

Grief doesn't go away—it becomes part of who we are. But amid it, there is a way to rest in the knowledge that your child is no longer suffering. They are whole, they are healed, and they are safe in the arms of God.

Though we long for them to be with us, there is comfort in knowing they have found a place free from pain, fear, and heartbreak. And one day, we will see them again.

A Promise of Reunion

That promise of reunion is the hope I hold onto every day. Until then, I trust God's plan and the peace He has given me through Bryant's complete healing. Whether your child's story ends on this earth or continues through survival, God's plan is perfect.

The peace we seek may not come quickly, but it is there, waiting to unfold as we lean into God's grace. And in that peace, we find strength, hope, and the courage to keep moving forward.

Chapter 24
FINDING JOY

"Grief reminds us of the depth of our love, and joy reminds us that love doesn't end, even when life does."

Grief is heavy. It can feel suffocating, leaving no room for lightness, laughter, or joy. In the early days after Bryant's death, the thought of smiling—let alone laughing—felt impossible. I couldn't imagine ever feeling happiness again. And even when I did, the guilt hit me like a punch to the gut. How could I find joy in a world where Bryant no longer existed?

I still remember the first time I laughed after he died. It wasn't anything extraordinary—just a funny story someone shared. But the moment the sound left my mouth, I wanted to return it. It felt like I was betraying him by daring to be happy while he was gone. The weight of that moment stayed with me for a long time.

I think that's something most grieving parents—or anyone mourning a loss—experience. There's an invisible line between sorrow and joy that feels impossible to cross, and even when you do, guilt yanks you right back. I spent so many days feeling like if I smiled, it meant I wasn't grieving hard enough—or maybe I wasn't honoring Bryant's memory the way I should have been.

But I've learned something important in the years since—joy and grief can coexist. Not only can they exist together, but they must. Joy doesn't dishonor our loved ones; it honors them by allowing us to carry the love and light they brought into our lives.

The Guilt That Comes with Moving Forward

Grief has a strange way of making time feel frozen. While the rest of the world keeps turning, you feel stuck in the moment everything changed. It's hard to imagine what moving forward looks like—and harder still to figure out how to do it without leaving your loved one behind. But over time, I realized joy didn't have to be an enemy of grief. It could be part of my healing.

Joy Doesn't Replace Grief—It Walks Alongside It

The truth is, joy and grief aren't opposites—they're partners. Grief reminds us of the depth of our love, and joy reminds us that love doesn't end, even when life does.

Bryant loved life. He found joy in the simplest things—cupcakes for nurses, late-night dinners at Waffle House, and laughter with friends. If he could see me now, I know he'd want me to keep living—not just existing. He'd like me to laugh, smile, and find beauty in the world the way he always did.

I will never forget one of the rare days we spent at home during Bryant's second year of cancer. By then, both my parents had passed. I was struggling with my grief for them while trying to stay positive and strong for Bryant. But as had happened many times before, my son was the one who comforted me and taught me so much about life and death. I was reeling in grief as I sat in silence in the living room. Bryant looked at me and then pointed to the front door.

"Do you see that door right there?" he asked. *"There's a whole world out there, Mom, and you need to get out there and live it. Because I'm dying and won't always be here, I'm going out that door to live as much as I can before it's too late. There are people out there who need you."*

That realization didn't happen overnight for me. It took time, and it's still something I have to remind myself of often. But I've learned that healing doesn't mean leaving grief behind; it means learning to carry it differently.

I still have days when sadness feels heavier than joy. Birthdays, anniversaries, and holidays still sting. But I've also learned to let those moments be what they are—a mix of sorrow and celebration, pain and love.

Practical Steps for Rediscovering Joy

> *"I still have days when sadness feels heavier than joy."*

For those struggling to find joy after loss, here are some practical ways I've learned to embrace happiness again:

1. **Celebrate their memory** – Don't be afraid to include your loved one in celebrations. Bake their favorite dessert, visit their favorite restaurant, or light a candle in their honor.

2. **Surround yourself with safe people** – Spend time with those who let you talk about your loved one without discomfort—people who allow you to cry and laugh in the same conversation.

3. **Create new traditions** – Build routines that honor your loved one while helping you move forward. For me, celebrating Bryant's birthday with Austin's family has become a cherished tradition.

4. **Allow yourself to feel grief and joy** – Don't push away happiness when it comes. Embrace it as a gift, not a betrayal.

5. **Give yourself grace** – Healing isn't linear. There will be setbacks, and that's okay. Allow yourself to take steps forward without guilt.

Let Joy and Grief Walk Together

I've learned that grief doesn't erase joy, and joy doesn't erase grief. They walk together, hand in hand. Grief reminds me of how deeply I loved Bryant, and joy reminds me that love never dies.

While writing this chapter, I'm reminded of another time Bryant spoke matter-of-factly about his upcoming death. He had accepted it with certainty for a year.

"Mom, have you thought about what you will do when I'm not around anymore?"

I tried to change the conversation as I always did because I couldn't accept how certain he was that he was dying. But in true Bryant fashion, he made sure I heard and understood what he was saying.

"I'm going to tell you what you need to do," Bryant continued. *"You need to keep writing. Even if you can't get your job back at the Ledger, I don't read everything you write, but you're good at it and must keep writing."*

His big, beautiful, contagious smile beamed as he spoke those words to me. Sadly, I couldn't write for some time after losing Bryant, but I think he would be incredibly proud of me now—because I can't stop writing.

So when joy comes knocking, let it in. Let it sit alongside the grief. Let it remind you that real, lasting love always finds a way to shine through the darkness.

A Message to Others Who Are Grieving

If you're in the early stages of grief, joy may feel impossible. And that's okay. Give yourself time. Be patient with your heart.

But when the day comes—and it will—when you smile or laugh again, don't feel guilty. Know that your joy doesn't mean you've stopped grieving.

It means you've found a way to carry your loved one with you as you continue to live. Happiness after loss isn't a betrayal; it's a testament to the love you shared. It's proof that their life mattered enough to keep shaping yours.

Bryant's story didn't end when he died, nor did mine. I'm still here. I'm still living. And I still carry his light—one smile at a time.

It doesn't mean the night will never come again. But it does mean that joy is still possible, even in the shadow of grief.

So keep walking. Keep living. Keep smiling. Your story—and your loved one's story—is far from over.

Chapter 25
FINDING FREEDOM IN FORGIVENESS

"The cracks from my past were still there, and the absence of the support I longed for during his illness magnified those old wounds."

Grief doesn't just come from death—it comes from broken trust, betrayal, and the unraveling of relationships we once believed would last forever. For me, grief began long before Bryant's diagnosis. It started with a marriage that left me feeling abandoned—emotionally and spiritually—at a time when I needed support the most.

The events surrounding my pregnancy with Bryant and the first months of his life were overshadowed by heartbreak. My marriage was crumbling, and the betrayal I experienced during that season planted seeds of pain and anger that stayed with me for years. Even after the divorce, the wounds remained.

When Bryant was diagnosed with cancer, I poured every ounce of myself into caring for him. But the cracks from my past were still there, and the absence of the support I had longed for during his illness only magnified those old wounds.

As a single mom, I felt the weight of every decision, every sleepless night, and every complicated conversation. It was a battle I faced largely alone. And while Bryant's faith strengthened mine, the anger I carried threatened to consume me.

Thanksgiving Night: A Breaking Point

Everything came to a head on Thanksgiving night—the night before Bryant died. He had been unresponsive all day. Emotions were raw, and grief hung thick in the air. In those moments, I found myself at odds with Bryant's dad.

The tension between us surfaced when I told him not to cry in front of Bryant, as he rested his head on the head rail of Bryant's bed weeping. The doctors had said to me that Bryant could still hear us, and I was afraid it would make him sad in his final hours before he left for heaven. He had told me repeatedly how much it hurt him to hear me cry after losing my parents. But his dad didn't know that, so he immediately became defensive, screaming at me that I couldn't tell him not to cry for his son. Thankfully, I convinced him to step into Bryant's restroom as the situation escalated.

The frustration, the pain, and the years of unspoken resentment surfaced at the worst possible time. I felt cheated again—just as I had during my pregnancy and the first months of Bryant's life. The last night I would ever sleep next to my son was overshadowed by even more hurt and anger.

We both screamed hurtful words in that bathroom, some that still to this day could be proven as lies.

Afterward, I struggled with all of these emotions—not just over those final moments with my ex but over the years leading up to them. I wrestled with questions I couldn't answer and pain I didn't know how to process. But in time, God began to soften my heart.

God's Quiet Intervention

For years, I carried so much hurt and anger—anger that slowly turned into bitterness. I replayed conversations, had terrible dreams, regretted words spoken in pain, and allowed those emotions to build walls around my heart.

After the divorce, we maintained a tolerable relationship for the boys' sake. There was a period after Bryant's death when I had to rely on his dad for financial help—especially when unexpected expenses came up like my car breaking down. Asking for help was beyond brutal, but in my grief, I couldn't see another way. I was highly grateful for his support and expressed that, especially when he didn't ask me to pay him back.

But at the same time, on one such occasion, he twisted my words and told our son his version of the story, which made Austin angry with me. I was always made to look bad. I knew I couldn't depend on or trust him more than I could when we were married. And I knew I'd never be able to move on if I kept turning to him. That was the last time I would turn to him for help.

I wanted closure. I needed closure.

I didn't realize I needed something even more—freedom. Freedom from the weight I had been carrying for far too long.

God began working in my heart before I even recognized it. He led me to a church I had once written for and loved deeply. It became a place of healing and restoration—a refuge where God could begin to chip away at my pain.

I joined two different 13-week Bible studies focused on divorce care and recovery. At first, I wasn't sure if they were the right fit, especially since I had been divorced for nearly two decades. But God made it clear—I needed to start at the beginning. If I ever wanted to move forward, I had to confront the wounds I had buried deeply.

Through those classes, I formed friendships with others who understood the devastation of broken relationships and the struggle to rebuild. Slowly, God showed me that healing wasn't about erasing the past but releasing its hold on me.

Forgiveness: The Key to Freedom

The turning point came during a forgiveness session in the divorce class. I knew it was time. I had to let go—not because the person who hurt me deserved it, but because I deserved freedom.

Forgiveness wasn't about pretending the past didn't happen or excusing the pain I had endured. It was about surrendering that pain to God and trusting Him to carry it for me. It meant releasing the hurt and anger so they no longer controlled my heart.

That moment of surrender was life-changing. It felt as though a weight had been lifted off my shoulders. I was free—not just from the resentment I had held onto for so long but also from the pain that had kept me from fully healing.

Faith Renewed, Purpose Restored

With forgiveness came clarity. I began writing again—something I hadn't done in years. Inspired by my pastor's message about someone in the congregation being called to share their gift of writing in a book, I started working on a different project: Secrets in the Glass House: Growing Up in a Southern Baptist Preacher's Home. After a year of writing, I was only on Chapter 10 and struggled to write. After having my spirit crushed, unintentionally, regarding my book, I put it down and walked away for five months. I never picked it back up.

After those five months, God placed this book in my heart quickly. I was unsure if I was ready to share my grief so openly, but I obeyed God's call, and within five days, I had written 16 chapters! The words poured out in ways I can't humanly explain other than it was God. It was God's way of bringing purpose to my pain. Since the day it began, Dec. 23, 2024, this book now contains 29 chapters. Every time I thought I was done, God wasn't finished! I give him all the praise and glory for every word on these pages.

This book isn't just about Bryant's story. It's about healing. It's about finding hope after loss and peace after pain. It's about letting go of the things that weigh us down so we can walk freely.

Trust me when I say freedom feels fantastic, even in the depths of grief! I finally feel alive again. Renewed. I still have a massive hole in my heart, represented by my son's absence, but God has been so good to me, filling in the holes and gaps in my heart with his presence, love, and grace.

Chapter 26
YOU TRULY AREN'T ALONE

Grief isn't something you overcome—it's something you learn to live with. It doesn't follow a timeline or fade after a set number of days. Instead, it becomes part of who you are, shaping your perspective, deepening your compassion, and strengthening your faith.

As you reach the end of this book, I want you to remember that your journey doesn't end here. Whether you are still in the early, suffocating days of grief or further along—where joy and sadness intertwine—there is hope for healing and purpose in the pain.

This book began as my story, but I pray it has become a companion for yours—a reminder that you are not alone, even in your darkest moments. Grief often isolates, but you don't have to walk this road alone. God is always near; if you allow Him, He will send people to walk alongside you.

Seeking Support—You Don't Have to Do This Alone

One of the most life-changing decisions I made after Bryant died was joining a grief recovery group. Being surrounded by others who understood my pain and fears created a safe space for healing—a place where I didn't have to hide my tears or explain my emotions. If you're feeling stuck or overwhelmed, I encourage you to seek support through resources like *GriefShare*.

GriefShare is a Christ-centered support group designed specifically for people grieving the loss of a loved one. It offers weekly video seminars, small group discussions, and personal study materials.

Are you not ready to be in a group setting? That's okay. You can watch the videos on the *GriefShare* website, find a group in your area, or sign up for daily email encouragement to remind you that healing is possible—even if it doesn't feel like it right now.

I have since returned to a *GriefShare* group but haven't completed it. I rely heavily on my two workbooks, the daily emails I subscribe to, and the endless information and videos shared on the website. Being wholly inspired by God's word, *GriefShare* has been my most significant asset and blessing.

You can also contact local churches or counseling centers for additional support groups.

Counseling and Therapy

While faith and community are essential parts of healing, professional counseling can also be incredibly valuable. Grief affects every part of us—emotionally, physically, and spiritually. A licensed counselor can help you process your emotions, develop healthy coping strategies, and address areas where grief may have led to anxiety, depression, or hopelessness. Unfortunately, I could not connect with the two counselors I sought help from. They first handed me a blank piece of paper and a box of crayons and told me to draw a picture of my heart. That did not sit well with me! Of course, the heart I begrudgingly drew was nothing but torn and ripped black pieces.

I left feeling worse than I did before I walked in. The following week, I returned, and the same counselor had misplaced my file. I went to another, this time a female with a different group, and she handed me a coloring book featuring Bible verses. You can imagine what I felt at that moment. I told her I had no desire to do **anything, let alone color!** She told me that would change as I progressed through the book, and the goal was for the pictures to eventually be filled with "beautifully artistic pages of vibrant colors" as I worked through my grief! I tried to tell her all I felt and could see was black- a deep, dark black. She instructed me to color anyway. I tried. I did, but black was the only color I was drawn to. And I scribbled over the entire page(s). The vibrant colors I always loved were no longer a part of my life, and it made me angry to see them. Forget coloring neatly inside the lines. Why would I? And how could I when my life had been so far out of the lines for more than two years by then, and all I saw was nothing but a tangled maze of lines wrapped around each other being held by what the counselor called "complicated grief" because of the three deaths I experienced in such a short period.

Don't let my experience cause you to be afraid to seek professional help, though. Coloring may work for you. Our situations are entirely different. Asking for support doesn't mean you lack faith—it means you're human and committed to healing.

As I stated earlier in this chapter, the grief support group, *GriefShare*, is what ultimately worked for me. While it wasn't easy, as thousands of tears poured down my face in each session, and I was physically and emotionally drained at the end of each session, the benefit was knowing I wasn't as alone as I felt I was.

Content Warning: The following section contains references to prescription medication, including a discussion of addiction, withdrawal, and emotional health. Reader discretion is advised. This book is not intended as medical advice. Please consult a qualified healthcare professional for any medical concerns. If you or someone you love is struggling with medication dependency, know that help is available.

Prescription or Holistic Medicine

Seeking help is not a sign of weakness—it's an act of courage. For me, that help came in many forms: faith, counseling, supportive friends, and even prescription medication.

My longtime primary doctor prescribed me a low-dose nerve pill after losing my parents during Bryant's cancer fight. I was experiencing extreme anxiety. My entire body was in a constant, visible tremble. Nothing about life was normal anymore, and I was utterly overwhelmed.

The same shaking I experienced outwardly was also happening inside my body. It's difficult to understand unless you've been through it, but I could feel my insides trembling. It was horrible, and it only intensified after Bryant died.

The downside was the nerve pill prescribed to me was a highly addictive drug. Researching the drug was something I wasn't capable of doing until it was too late, and the damage was done. I continued taking it for two years after my son died. The medication helped take the edge off and allowed me to focus on necessary tasks, such as going back to work, and aided in my sleep, which was impaired. Looking back, I wish I had stopped sooner and properly, but instead, I was forced to quit suddenly and abruptly while working with FEMA in Miami.

The job with FEMA came quickly, and I never knew from one second to the next how long I would be out of town or even where I would be sent next. Because of that, I found myself in Miami for a month, and my prescription ran out, and because it was considered a narcotic, it couldn't be refilled. I was okay for the first couple of days without it, but when my body realized it was gone, I was thrust into a horrible physical and emotional state. Thankfully, by God's provision, I had completed all of my assigned work and was being paid to sit in a hotel to receive my next batch of work. It probably sounds like a dream to most, but it was a nightmare for me. My grief was still new and raw to me, and being alone was the worst thing for me. Then, add the sudden loss of the medicine to my system, which enabled me to function. There was no denying I was in trouble. I contacted a Facebook friend from home with family or friends nearby. I can't remember which or exactly how it played out. I know it resulted in me being connected to a local Southern Baptist church in Miami for assistance. A retired counselor from the church was sent to my hotel. Seeing a kind, helpful face relieved my aching heart, body, and disoriented mind. I can't remember her name, but she was terrific - a true God send. She listened and sat with me, refusing to leave me alone. After speaking with a doctor, it was decided it was not safe for me to be alone, so this angel of a lady jumped through hoops with my immediate boss with FEMA to get my rental car picked up, being I was in no shape to drive, my laptop and other FEMA equipment picked up at the hotel and persuaded them of the urgency to get me a flight back home, one-way, the same day. FEMA paid for all my travel, including flights, and sometimes it could take up to five days to get a flight approved. So, that action alone was proof of God's presence. She helped me pack, get to the airport, and get on the right flight where Austin was waiting on the receiving end in Pensacola.

The withdrawal and detox from the nerve pill lasted more than 17 days—a horrendous experience. I could have gotten more of the drug when I returned home, but after going through what I did in Miami, I didn't like how it made me feel. I didn't want to rely on it to survive. God was gracious, helping me through that period and restoring my well-being.

There's so much stigma around medication, and I worried it might dull my emotions or make me feel detached from the memories I was clinging to. It did help me initially in the depths of my pain from losing both my parents and continuing to fight for Bryant's life. It enabled me to do what I needed then, but I became dependent on it. When I realized in Miami what a wreck I honestly was without it, I knew I had to have help, and a narcotic nerve pill was not the help I thought I needed. I needed grace.

The nerve pill didn't take the grief away, but it gave me enough stability to start facing it. It allowed me to function, breathe, and take the first small steps toward healing. That's when I learned a vital truth: there's no shame in needing help—whether through a prescription, therapy, or simply talking to someone who understands. But it is crucial to understand highly addictive drugs are not the solution and can be deceiving, making you think you are okay when you genuinely are not. The medication I was taking only numbed my symptoms by calming me, but it did nothing for the heart of my grief. They only prolonged my healing.

To be completely transparent, I am on an anti-depressant that was prescribed a short time after Bryant was born. I was experiencing severe panic attacks triggered by the broken situation at home with my marriage that I chose to stay in for five more years. Only for the same patterns to continue. I hope to be free of that one day as my trust in God grows and strengthens.

Grief is personal, and no single solution works for everyone. But if you're struggling under its weight, I encourage you to consult your doctor or a counselor. Admitting you need support is a sign of strength, and finding the right tools to help you heal is a step toward freedom. God provides resources, and sometimes, medication can be one of them. Don't worry about what people say. They **will talk** and **will judge** you. Focus on the cross Jesus died upon **just for you.** That is where your healing will come from.

Practical Steps for Healing

Grief can feel overwhelming, but small steps can lead to significant changes over time. Here are some suggestions to help you keep moving forward:

1. **Start a Journal**. Write down your thoughts, prayers, and memories. Use it as a safe space to process your emotions and track your growth.

2. **Honor Their Memory**. Celebrate birthdays, anniversaries, and memorable moments by lighting a candle, visiting their favorite place, or donating to a cause they care about.

3. **Be Gentle with Yourself**. Don't rush the process. Healing takes time, and it's okay to step back from the pressure to "move on."

4. **Reconnect with Your Faith. Read scripture**, listen to worship music, and spend time in prayer. Let God meet you where you are—even in the messiness.

5. **Stay Connected**. Surround yourself with people who encourage and support you, whether friends, family, or grief group members.

A Personal Charge to You

If there's one thing I hope this book has shown you, grief is not the end of your story. It's complicated, messy, and life-altering—but it doesn't have to destroy you.

God created you for more than survival. He has a plan for your life, even amid sorrow. Trust Him to carry you through the darkness and into the light. Lean into His promises. Let Him be your strength when you have none of your own. And know it's okay to grieve and still hold on to hope.

The Journey Continues

Grief isn't something we finish—it's something we carry. But with God's grace and the support of others, we can carry it with strength and purpose.

I'll leave you with this thought—your loved one's story didn't end, and neither does yours. Keep their memory alive. Honor their life by continuing to live yours.

Let their legacy inspire you to love deeply, give generously, and trust fully in the God who walks beside you, even through the valley.

You are not alone. You are loved. And you are stronger than you know.

From One Broken Heart to Another,

Janet

Chapter 27
SCRIPTURE FOR THE JOURNEY

The Bible is such a beautiful book, written for all ages and situations. I've never been more thankful for God's Word than I am now. Every question I've had in my grief is answered in its pages. Every emotion I have felt and lived through has a scripture that speaks to it, bringing assurance, comfort, and even hope.

With technology as advanced as it is, many of us have moved away from holding a physical Bible, flipping through its delicate pages, and reading from it. That's okay—but during grief, you may find the book itself to be a source of deep comfort.

God's majesty and power are in those pages, waiting for you to dive in. If you read online, consider placing your Bible under your pillow at night. I did it out of sheer desperation, and it gave me a greater sense of security. Make it a constant companion—you will notice a difference.

When You Feel *Lost*

"Trust in the Lord with all your heart and lean not on your own understanding; in all your ways submit to Him, and He will make your paths straight." — Proverbs 3:5-6

Grief is complex and unique to each person's experience. Understanding it—and the many emotions it encompasses—can feel overwhelming. But this verse reminds us that God will guide you through the fog of grief and bring you understanding. Trust Him.

So do not fear, for I am with you; do not be dismayed, for I am your God. I will strengthen you and help you; I will uphold you with my righteous right hand." Isaiah 41:10

Loneliness is often a by-product of grief, but God assures you that you are never alone. He promises to be with you and to give you strength.

When Waves of Grief Drown You

"The Lord is close to the brokenhearted and saves those who are crushed in spirit." — *Psalm 34:18*

Grief can feel unbearable, but knowing God is near brings comfort. He is present in our pain and offers healing for your broken heart.

" "Come to me, all you who are weary and burdened, and I will give you rest. Take my yoke upon you and learn from me, for I am gentle and humble in heart, and you will find rest for your souls." — Matthew 11:28-30

God promises rest and relief for your weary soul. He invites you to lay your burdens at His feet.

When You Need Strength to Keep Going

"But those who hope in the Lord will renew their strength. They will soar on wings like eagles; they will run and not grow weary, they will walk and not be faint." — Isaiah 40:31

Placing hope in God will renew your strength and sustain you through the journey.

"I can do all things through Christ who strengthens me." Philippians 4:13

Even in our darkest moments of weakness, God gives us the strength to keep moving forward.

When You Feel Alone

"Be strong and courageous. Do not be afraid or terrified because of them, for the Lord your God goes with you; He will never leave you nor forsake you." — Deuteronomy 31:6

No matter how alone you feel, God is always with you. He is constant and unshakable.

"Even though I walk through the darkest valley, I will fear no evil, for You are with me; Your rod and Your staff, they comfort me." — Psalm 23:4

God walks beside you in your darkest moments, carrying you with His comfort and protection.

When You Need Hope for the Future

"For I know the plans I have for you," declares the Lord, *"plans to prosper you and not to harm you, plans to give you a hope and a future."* — *Jeremiah 29:11*

Even when we struggle to understand God's plans, we are reminded that His plans are good. He offers hope for the future.

"And we know that in all things God works for the good of those who love Him, who have been called according to His purpose." — *Romans 8:28*

Even in tragedy, God is working behind the scenes for our ultimate good and His glory.

When You Need Comfort

God is the source of all comfort. He not only heals our hearts but also equips us to comfort others in their struggles. One day, He will remove all pain and sorrow—our ultimate comfort in eternity.

"He will wipe every tear from their eyes. There will be no more death or mourning or crying or pain, for the old order of things has passed away." — *Revelation 21:4*

When You Seek Joy and Renewal

"For His anger lasts only a moment, but His favor lasts a lifetime; weeping may stay for the night, but rejoicing comes in the morning." — *Psalm 30:5*

This verse acknowledges the reality of grief but assures us that joy will return. It reminds us of God's enduring faithfulness and the promise of better days ahead.

"The joy of the Lord is your strength." — *Nehemiah 8:10*

Joy may seem impossible in the midst of grief, but God Himself is our strength. His joy sustains us, even when we feel weak.

"You have turned my mourning into dancing; you have removed my sackcloth and clothed me with joy." — *Psalm 30:11*

God has the power to transform even our deepest sorrow into joy. Over time, He brings healing and restoration.

"Those who sow in tears will reap with songs of joy." — *Psalm 126:5*

God sees our sorrow and, in His perfect timing, will bring joy and blessings.

The Bible is rich with wisdom and comfort for those who grieve. Many books speak directly to the emotions that accompany loss, offering understanding, healing, and hope. Here are some key books and passages that address different aspects of grief:

1. Psalms - Expressing Raw Emotions

The Psalms are filled with raw, honest emotions—grief, despair, and ultimately, hope in God.

Psalm 147:3 – "He heals the brokenhearted and binds up their wounds."

Psalm 42:3, 11 – The psalmist mourns deeply, asking, "Why, my soul, are you downcast? Why so disturbed within me?"—yet ultimately chooses to hope in God.

2. Lamentations – Mourning Deep Loss

Written after the destruction of Jerusalem, Lamentations expresses profound sorrow and grief, yet it also reminds us of God's faithfulness in the midst of suffering.

Lamentations 3:22-23 – "Because of the Lord's great love, we are not consumed, for His compassions never fail. They are new every morning; great is Your faithfulness."

3. Job – Wrestling with Suffering and Grief

Job endured immense loss—his children, wealth, and health. In his grief, he wrestled with God, searching for meaning and questioning His plan.

Job 1:21 – "The Lord gave, and the Lord has taken away; blessed be the name of the Lord."

Job 19:25-26 – "Even in his despair, Job declares, 'I know that my Redeemer lives."

4. Ecclesiastes - The Fleeting Nature of Life

Solomon Reflects on Life's Brevity and the Inevitability of Loss

Ecclesiastes 3:1, 4 – "There is a time for everything, a time to weep and a time to laugh, a time to mourn and a time to dance."

5. Isaiah – God's Comfort and Promise

Isaiah 41:10 – "Do not fear, for I am with you; do not be dismayed, for I am your God. I will strengthen you and help you."

Isaiah 53:3-4 – "Jesus is described as a man of sorrows, acquainted with grief."

6. John - Jesus' Compassion for the Grieving

When Lazarus died, Jesus grieved, showing His deep empathy for our sorrow.

John 11:35 – *"Jesus wept."*

John 16:22 – *"Now is your time of grief, but I will see you again, and you will rejoice."*

7 Corinthians – God's Comfort in Our Suffering

2 Corinthians 1:3-4 – *"Praise be to the God and Father of our Lord Jesus Christ, the Father of compassion and the God of all comfort, who comforts us in all our troubles so that we can comfort those in any trouble with the comfort we ourselves receive."*

"These scriptures acknowledge the deep pain of grief while reminding us of God's presence, His compassion, and His promise of restoration."

Chapter 28
ENCOURAGEMENT FOR THE BROKENHEARTED

Grief is not the end of your story. To the grieving mother, father, sibling, spouse, or friend who has walked through unimaginable loss—I want you to know this: you are not alone.

There is no manual for grief, no perfect roadmap that shows you how to move forward after losing someone you love. But there is hope. There is healing. And there is life after loss.

I have walked through so many valleys—losing my grandparents, my niece Reagan, my friend's son Travis, who felt like my own, my parents, and then my son, Bryant. Each loss left me broken in different ways. Each one tested my faith.

And with Bryant, I didn't know if I would ever recover.

God's Presence in the Pain

There were so many moments when I questioned God—why He allowed this to happen, why He didn't step in to save Bryant, and why He let me endure so much loss. I didn't always get the answers I wanted, but what I did get was God's presence.

Even in my darkest hours—whether lying beside Bryant in the hospital, crying in the shower, or standing at the edge of the Gulf, wondering if I could go on—God was there.

He didn't leave me alone in my grief, and He won't leave you alone either.

On **November 17, 2016**, Bryant was admitted to the hospital for the final time, in the same room where it all began. He passed away on **November 25, 2016**—the morning after Thanksgiving.

At first, I thought it was just a painful coincidence that so many of these dates aligned. But as time passed, I realized it wasn't a coincidence at all. God arranged them so I couldn't miss or deny the truth: He had a plan. And all these years later, He has reminded me again.

On October 26, 2023—one day before the anniversary of Bryant's diagnosis—my son, Austin, got married. And then, just eight years after Bryant's passing, on October 7, 2024, my first grandbaby was born.

God knew

He knew how deep my pain was. He knew how much my broken heart needed reminders of His faithfulness. And in the midst of my deepest sorrow, He was already writing a story of redemption.

Had I given in to the thoughts of suicide that haunted me in the early years after Bryant's passing, I would have missed this:

- I would have missed watching my son find love.
- I would have missed holding my first grandbaby in my arms.
- I would have missed God's way of telling me, "I am still here, and I am not finished with your story."

A Purpose Beyond the Pain

Bryant's life wasn't long, but it was enough to fulfil, God's purpose. His faith, courage, and kindness touched countless lives, and his story continues to inspire others today. I believe God gives purpose to our pain—He doesn't waste a single tear. And as much as it hurts, He can use even the deepest grief to bring something beautiful from the ashes.

Maybe your purpose is to share your story. Maybe it's to comfort others who are hurting. Or maybe it's simply to keep showing up each day as a testament to God's faithfulness, even when the road is hard.

A Call to the Brokenhearted

If you're reading this and feel broken, I want you to know:

- You don't have to be strong all the time. Let yourself cry. Let yourself feel the pain. Healing begins when we're honest about where we are.
- You don't have to rush your healing. Grief has no timeline, and there's no "right" way to mourn. Take it one day—one breath—at a time.

You don't have to have all the answers. God's shoulders are big enough for your questions, doubts, and fears.

You don't have to do this alone. Lean on your faith, your family, and your friends. Surround yourself with people who understand and love you through it.

You don't have to give up hope. Even when it feels impossible, trust that God can redeem your story.

You Were Made for More

I know what it's like to feel like giving up. I know what it is to stand at the water's edge and want to keep walking until the waves pull you under.

But I also know what it's like to step back—to let God pull you out of the darkness. To keep living even when it hurts. Because that's what Bryant wanted for me.

Over and over again, in those two years of fighting, he told me, "Mom, you have to keep going. You have to keep living." He tried his best to make me promise—something I couldn't do until the ride back to the condo, the last one we would ever take.

Bryant knew his battle would end before mine did. But he never wanted his death to be the end of my story. He wanted me to live. And if he were here today, I know his unforgettable smile would shine brighter than ever. Not just because of all his fight accomplished—the awareness, the love, the lives his story touched—but because of life itself.

Because his brother, Austin, has built a beautiful life. Because a new generation—his niece, Ava Jane—has entered the world. Because I kept going, even when I didn't think I could.

I can picture him grinning, shaking his head at me, saying, *"See, Mom! I told you. You had to keep living."*

And he was right.

Even in grief and pain, life keeps going. Love keeps going. God keeps working. And as long as I have breath, I will keep going too. Because Bryant's story isn't over. And neither is mine.

If you've walked this road of grief and felt alone—if you've questioned where God is in your pain, if you're searching for peace that feels just out of reach—I want you to know there is hope.

There is a God who loves you. A Savior who understands suffering because He endured it Himself.

A Prayer for the Brokenhearted

Dear Heavenly Father,

I lift every grieving heart reading these words to You. I pray that You wrap them in Your comfort, hold them in Your arms, and remind them that they are never alone. Give them the strength to face each day, the courage to keep going, and the faith to trust in Your plan—even when it hurts. Let them know their pain has a purpose and that You will bring beauty from the ashes.

In Jesus' name, Amen.

Chapter 29
BRYANT'S GREATEST HOPE

Through it all—his fight, his suffering, his final days—Bryant never lost faith. He knew where he was going. He had peace in knowing that death wasn't the end; it was just the beginning of eternity with Jesus.

Bryant didn't fear dying because he had complete confidence in his salvation. And more than anything, he wanted that same peace for others. I remember conversations where he talked about the importance of pressing forward, living life, and trusting in God. But even deeper than that, I know he wanted everyone he loved to know Jesus as he did.

That's why I want to share this with you. If you're reading this—searching for hope, feeling lost in grief, or wondering where God is—let me tell you what Bryant knew: God is right here. He loves you. And He wants you to have the same peace that carried Bryant through his most challenging days.

If Bryant were sitting here right now, he'd say it with his unforgettable smile: "It's gonna be okay. God's got this." And I believe he'd want you to know that you, too, can have that same assurance, faith, and hope.

Bryant accepted Jesus as his Lord and Savior long before he was baptized. Because my dad—Bryant's Papa—had baptized me, his brother, and Meredith, it was only natural that Bryant wanted his Papa to baptize him as well.

After waiting for his papa to be well enough to baptize him due to his poor health, Bryant decided he couldn't wait any longer. He approached my dad with an idea, almost as if he had a sense of what was to come in just a few short months.

"Papa, I really want to be baptized, and since you aren't strong enough to do it, I was thinking you could do the talking, and Bro. Tim (his youth pastor) could do the dunking."

We all got a good laugh at his choice of words and his idea. So, on **May 11, 2014**—just five months before his cancer was discovered—his papa did the "talking," and his youth pastor did the "dunking" in the same church my dad pastored for ten years, where he had also baptized his other grandchildren. The same church where Bryant's funeral was held two years later. It was a beautiful moment in all of our lives and a truly special day.

We had no idea how that moment would fit into Bryant's life story or how his faith would carry him through his fight, his passing, and even beyond. Here is the knowledge that led Bryant to be baptized that day—something he deeply wanted you to know, in hopes that you, too, could find the same peace he did.

1. Recognize Your Need For God

We all fall short of His holiness, and sin creates a barrier between us and God.

Romans 3:23 (NIV) – *"For all have sinned and fall short of the glory of God."*

Isaiah 59:2 (ESV) – *"But your iniquities have made a separation between you and your God."*

2. Understand the Cost of Sin

The consequence of sin is death, but God offers us the gift of eternal life through Jesus.

Romans 6:23 (NIV) – *"For the wages of sin is death, but the gift of God is eternal life in Christ Jesus our Lord."*

3. Believe That Jesus Paid the Price for You

Jesus took the punishment we deserved by dying on the cross.

Romans 5:8 (NIV) – *"But God demonstrates His own love for us in this: While we were still sinners, Christ died for us."*

John 3:16 (ESV) – *"For God so loved the world, that He gave His only Son, that whoever believes in Him should not perish but have eternal life."*

4. Confess and Trust in Jesus as Lord

Salvation cannot be earned—it is a gift from God, received through faith.

Romans 10:9 (NIV) – *"If you declare with your mouth, 'Jesus is Lord,' and believe in your heart that God raised Him from the dead, you will be saved."*

Ephesians 2:8-9 (ESV) – *"For by grace you have been saved through faith, not a result of works, so that no one may boast."*

5. Accept Jesus and Let Him Transform Your Life

When you put your trust in Jesus, He makes you new.

2 Corinthians 5:17 (NIV) – *"Therefore, if anyone is in Christ, the new creation has come: The old has gone, the new is here!"*

John 1:12 (ESV) – *"But to all who did receive Him, who believed in His name, He gave the right to become children of God."*

How to Receive Christ

You can accept Jesus right now, just as Bryant did, by praying a simple prayer like this:

"Lord Jesus, I know that I am a sinner. I believe You died for my sins and rose again. I ask You to forgive me, come into my life, and be my Lord and Savior. I trust in You alone for my salvation. Thank You for loving me and giving me eternal life. Amen."

Next Steps

If you prayed to receive Christ, here are some next steps:

Read the Bible daily to grow in your faith.

Pray and talk to God regularly.

Find a Bible-believing church for fellowship and encouragement.

Share your faith with someone you trust.

You are not alone in your grief, and you are not alone in this journey of faith. God is with you, and His love will carry you through.

Helpful Bible Study Resources

Spending time in God's Word is essential for growing in faith, especially during difficult seasons. If you're not sure where to start, here are some free and easy-to-use Bible apps:

YouVersion Bible App – Offers NIV, ESV, many other translations, devotionals, and reading plans. www.bible.com

First 5 - A devotional app that helps you start each day in God's Word. www.first5.org

Solid Joys - Daily devotionals by John Piper, rooted in Scripture. www.desiringgod.org/solid-joys

Blue Letter Bible - Provides in-depth study tools, including Greek and Hebrew word studies. www.blueletterbible.org

Bible Gateway - An excellent tool for reading and listening to the Bible, with additional study resources. www.biblegateway.com

Through the Word - Guided chapter-by-chapter Bible audio teachings. www.throughtheword.org

These tools can help you dive deeper into Scripture—whether you're seeking comfort, answers, or simply looking to grow in your faith.

Bryant's Final Gift

At Bryant's funeral, miniature wooden crosses were given out at the close of the service as a symbol of his faith, strength, and greatest hope.

As I stood before the large crowd and shared Bryant's desire for everyone to know Jesus, his friends quietly moved through the packed church, handing out these small but powerful reminders of the faith he carried until his last breath.

Each person left that day with a piece of Bryant's legacy in their hands, a reminder that his fight was never just about cancer. It was about faith. It was about Jesus and the cross. In his last weeks on earth, Bryant's greatest prayer was that others would find the same unshakable hope he had. I still get messages from people who were there and received a cross. They come on the darkest of days, giving me renewed strength.

This photo was taken after Bryant's funeral - a moment frozen in time. A friend I met in the hospital, as she, too, was a cancer mom, captured this picture of her son, a cancer survivor & one of Bryant's friends, holding one of those crosses after attending Bryant's funeral.

A beautiful reminder of the life Bryant lived and the legacy he left us with.

PART 5

MEMORIES IN PICTURES

Bryant Thomas Cooper

Bryant was a country boy through and through. He loved John Deere tractors, a love that began as a toddler riding on his Papa Cooper's tractor. Before getting sick, he started working at Smith Tractor, a longtime John Deere dealership owned by family friend **Ricky Smith**. Ricky had grown up working alongside my Papa Little in the dealership. He got Bryant a John Deere uniform while he was sick, something Bryant dreamed of. The above picture is a selfie Bryant took of himself out on a call with friend **Tab Jernigan** after being diagnosed. He was so proud! It was only fitting that Bryant was buried in it and his hat.

The Tide Was Good to Bryant

Bryant liked football; his favorite college team was the Alabama Crimson Tide. On some of his worst days, Former Coach Nick Saban, his wife Terri, and former players AJ McCarron and Trent Richardson were highlights for Bryant.

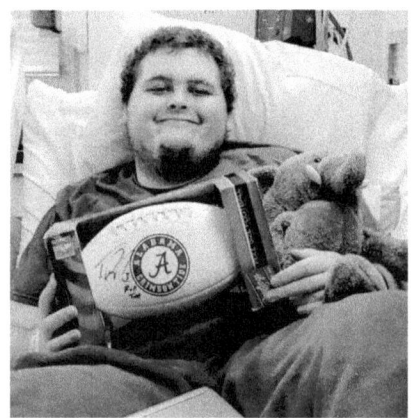

Prom 2015 - 5 months after diagnosis

March 2015- Our preacher's daughter, *Cheyenne Redditt*, asked Bryant to prom with her. I'm so thankful for the pictures *Rhonda Lassiter* took at the Smith Tractor dealership where Bryant worked before getting sick. He was grateful for the photo of two of his favorite things - John Deere tractors and Tahoe.

Reagan and Bryant

All of these pictures were taken two weeks before Bryant's cousin, Reagan, died unexpectedly. She and Bryant didn't have much time together, but I know they are in Heaven with my parents, their Granny, and Papa. They shared a special bond and loved each other fiercely. Reagan was his protector.

WHAT EVERY GRIEVING MOTHER WISHES YOU KNEW

Lcpl. Travis M. Nelson

8/05/92 - 8/18/11

Friends Through it All

Bryant was blessed with so many good friends. Friends that stuck with him through it all. I'm so thankful for this specific circle of friends and how they loved my son.

WHAT EVERY GRIEVING MOTHER WISHES YOU KNEW

When Friends Become Family

Garry and *Vicki Baggett's* home became a second home to Bryant before he was diagnosed. He and their son, Corry, had a friendship steeped in a love for hunting, football, and fast vehicles. The Baggetts became the family unit I couldn't give Bryant after divorce and a time of inner struggle. They kept him in church when I couldn't. I'm forever grateful for the love they shared with us.

Kena and Bryant

Bryant and Kena met in the hospital when she was only 11 months old and he was 17, but their age difference didn't matter. They were best friends in and out of the hospital.

WHAT EVERY GRIEVING MOTHER WISHES YOU KNEW

Johann Doum

Oct. 11, 2000 - Nov. 23, 2016

Three families brought together in the hospital by cancer

Five children all fighting cancer at the same time in the same hospital. Five out of five died. Rachel was the first of our group to die on November 19, 2015, followed by Jace on Nov. 28, 2015. Kena died 10 months later, followed by Johann and Bryant two months later. Childhood Cancer is not rare.

Our Hospital Family

We couldn't have asked for better care from the Studer Family Children's Hospital nurses and staff at Ascension Sacred Heart Hospital. Bryant loved all of them.

My Family 2025

My oldest son, Austin, got married in October of 2023, and not only did I gain a daughter-in-law, Lorri, but two special little girls, Ella & Lakelyn. And then along came Ava Jane, born in October 2024.

WHAT EVERY GRIEVING MOTHER WISHES YOU KNEW

Celebrating Bryant

We celebrated Bryant's 28th Birthday on Feb. 23, 2025. My daughter-in-law and photographer, Lorri, took these beautiful pictures of her and Austin's baby, Ava Jane, with Bryant's picture.

Because of how Ava reacted when seeing a larger version of this picture the week before Bryant's birthday, we believe she knows Bryant. She has the same reaction each time and has the same response in a video we showed her of Bryant talking.

THIS BOOK IS A TRIBUTE TO THE FOLLOWING PEOPLE WHO WERE A BIG PART OF OUR STORY

To my parents, Rev. Thomas Little, Jr., and Joyce Carnley Little-

I owe my life to you. I couldn't have wished for better parents than you. Thank you for leaving behind not just words of wisdom but a foundation of faith that continues to guide me. Dad, your sermons have been a source of strength, helping me navigate this journey of grief and healing. You always wanted us to write a book together, so this is for you, Dad. I hope this book honors your and Mom's extraordinary legacy of faithfulness, wisdom, integrity, and shared love for God and people.

To my niece, Reagan-

You were the first loss that shattered our family. Your passing left us heartbroken, but the precious memories of your beautiful face, spirit, and feisty personality will always be a light in the darkness. Bryant loved you fiercely, and now you are together in Heaven. Your story will always be a part of ours.

To Travis, our Marine, and Heroe

You were the one person who could frustrate me the most but also make me belly laugh. I have so many fun memories of you and my boys. I'll always be proud of you, Travis. You never backed down from a challenge and served us all so well. Missing you hurts, but I'm thankful you and Bryant are together in Heaven.

To sweet Rachel-

You were the first of our hospital family to leave for Heaven. The halls were dimmer when you left as you lit up every face that met you and filled our hearts with love and laughter. You are so missed.

To sweet Jace-

I still see your beautiful smile and hear your sweet voice. I'll never forget when you asked Bryant if a particular procedure hurt. It still breaks my heart. You were so brave, Jace. I know Bryant is with you in Heaven, which makes me smile.

To our sunshine in the storm, Kena-

Oh, precious, beautiful Kena, the words are hard to find. You were like a soothing balm for our fears and aching hearts. What I'd give to hold you one more time or hear your sweet baby voice call out for 'Byant 'or "dip it.' Thank you for being our literal sunshine in such a horrific storm. I will always love you.

To Adventurous Johann-

I'm so sorry you had to suffer the way you did in the end. No one deserves the ravages of cancer, especially not you. We were opposites; you were quiet and me loud, but you had such a sweet, generous spirit. I love your adventurous spirit and love for different foods. You are so missed and loved.

Acknowledgments

I express my deepest gratitude to the incredible nurses and doctors at **Studer Family Children's Hospital at Ascension Sacred Heart in Pensacola, FL.** Your unwavering dedication, compassion, and love for Bryant and our family will never be forgotten. A special thank you to nurses **Jessica Faith Johnson, Tanya Biggs, Kayla Olson, Laura Crawford Blanchet, Megan Daniel Bratton, Kumi Dryster, Katie Kennedy, Anna Westerman, and Haley Hanson—nurses who not only tenderly and devotionally cared for Bryant** but also cared for me in ways that went far beyond their professional roles. There are more who moved on to other departments or states who were also with us for a portion of the journey. Whether taking their breaks, including lunch, in Bryant's hospital room, cooking meals for us, or taking Bryant downstairs to Wendy's or Subway when they felt he needed a break, their kindness knew no bounds. They loved Bryant and me so well and will forever hold a special place in my heart.

To **Dr. Jeffrey Schwartz**, thank you for the care, humor, and connection you shared with Bryant. Of all the oncologists, Bryant loved you most. From joking about Bryant's ability to grow a full beard even after chemo (when you couldn't) to bonding over vehicles—Bryant proudly showing off his loaded truck with jacked-up wheels while you teased about driving a Mini Cooper—you gave him moments of joy amid hardship. We are forever grateful for your dedication extended to Bryant, Kena, and Johann.

To Sacred Heart employees and one-of-a-kind **Traniece Williams, a.k.a. Miss T** and **Celine**, you were bright lights for Bryant and me every day with your outgoing personalities and generous spirits. Thank you for bringing smiles to Bryant's face and standing with us even away from the hospital.

To **Jeff Hendrix,** a fellow cancer parent, and his former neighbor, **Cindi Bear Bonner**, for spearheading the creation of **Rally Gulf Coast**, a non-profit organization for patients and families affected by childhood cancer which operates out of the Studer Family Children's Hospital in Pensacola. Rally Gulf Coast is under the umbrella of the Rally Foundation in Atlanta. Both work tirelessly to raise funds for more research in childhood cancer and the drugs needed to treat the children. The Pensacola group began during Bryant's treatment and continues to make a difference today for other cancer families. Thank you for being such a tremendous help to our family and many others. Your support provided strength, hope, and practical assistance when we needed it most. This organization is a worthwhile place to support with your tax-free donations. The money is indeed used for local children.

I would also like to thank the Cordova Mall **Chick-fil-A owner, Kathy Worley,** for providing meals to everyone in the Oncology Unit every Tuesday night in the hospital. Sometimes, this was the first food of the day for us. As far as I know, she still does this. It is such an incredible act of love and generosity. One of her former employees, **Matthew Bailey**, a teenager at the time, graciously served each of us and quickly learned that sweet tea was Bryant's favorite. He often left Bryant with an entire gallon, knowing it was sometimes all he could stomach. Matthew is now a pharmacist, but his kindness during that time left a lasting impression on our hearts.

To **all the local churches—and even those farther away—who prayed continuously and supported us**, thank you for surrounding us with love and faith. Your prayers and generosity sustained us through the darkest days. Special thanks to **Rev. Delbert Redditt** and **Brother Mitch Herring** for always being there for us. Bryant loved you both dearly.

Finally, to the countless individuals who stepped in to help in ways big and small—bringing meals, running errands, innumerable gifts for Bryant, and simply being present—your acts of kindness and compassion made an immeasurable impact on our lives. This book would never end if I listed you all by name. I've mentioned some in the book, but please know your role was just as important to me and Bryant and didn't go unnoticed.